I0104064

ACKNOWLEDGEMENTS

This book is my version of a training manual for police and community members in the wake of shooting and choking of unarmed black men. As Common lyrics attest, there is nothing that ever changes in our neighborhoods. Marvin Gayle shared the same concern in his hit record, "Inner City Blues, Makes You Want Holler". And so did Stevie, when he sung, "Living for The City". As a product of the concrete matrix, I am committed to share my assessment and suggestions to anyone willing to listen. Based on the two millions black inmates that have forfeited their freedom, it appears that an alternative voice needs to be heard because we are not reaching those that we need to reached the most.

This training manual offers information and tools that CEOs of major corporations use daily to make their companies become more competitive and productive. Why not share the same information with "Ordinary people" who may need it more. This manual includes a schematic of how the brain works under stress which if understood can be the difference between life, imprisonment, or even death. I offer this training because its' my obligation. To whom much is given, much is required: Luke 12:48, and to "Speak up for those who cannot speak for themselves, for the rights of all who are destitute…Speak up and judge fairly; defend the rights of the poor and needy: Proverbs 31:8-9. This manual is not intented to offend but it may present material that challenges an individual to think beyond their socialized beliefs. And in that case, it focuses on personal growth and development.

The book is dedicated to Coco, my soul mate, who puts up with me. My beautiful Daughter, Minister Jonquia Vaulx and her husband, Jay, and my awesome grandchildren, Jada, Jayla, and James, Jr. This book/training is also dedicated to my favorite cousin "Mulch" Mays, my black history teacher, Gloria Cotton, Rueben Rodriguez, who got me into Calumet College, and Thomas Barnes, Former Gary Mayor, Police Brothers, Booker Blumenberg, Roy Rice, Sal Haymon, Gerald Clayton, Robert Fleece, Richard Ligon, Attorney James Cook, and all the "corner boys". Through them, I learned what integrity and loyalty meant. And of course, I want to acknowledge my academic sisters Dr. Jonella Bradford, mentor and Dr. Melanie Smith, who contributed to research and training on emotional intelligence. In addition, I want to acknowledge my late parents Red and Mabel Hall, and my late Cherokee grandmother, Snowz Curtis. And special thanks to Civil Rights Activist, Margie Phelps. These are my Giants, and I will always be indebted to them for their counsel and tough love. I, also, want to acknowledge my Pastors who are always there to motivate me.

Mucho Gracias.

For Training, Workshops, Consulting, or Seminars, Contact me:

Dr. John "Jay" Hall
Leading with Integrity
1710 Saddle Creek Dr.
Houston, Texas 77090
Ph.# 832-886-9370
Email: Jayearl2007@yahoo.com

Foreward

This training manual was created based on a recognition that most officers enter law enforcement with a naïve understanding of the requirements of the job. Officers learn how to perform their jobs from their peers and supervisors. Hence, police officers are socialized into the police culture. The "We" versus "Them" is part of that culture. It is the sincere desire of the writer of this manual to bridge the chasm that currently exist between the police and the community they serve. The implication of the "We" versus "Them" mentality is that the police are at war with some communities all the time. We believe it is this perception that is hindering positive police community relations. This manual provides training to examine not only this mental model held by some police officers, but also the perception of the police held by some communities.

We recognize the "We" versus "Them" mentality is a response to the difficult job that police officers face. Police officers are routinely required to make split second decisions that rules and regulations do not always address. When police officer's response to volatile situations, they carry an emotional history which can become a crucial aspect of their decision making process. Making the right decision during a highly charged situation demands strength of character, because the immediacy of the situation may blur the line between right and wrong choices. Police officers can and do, make mistakes.

In an effort to address this chasm, a new mental construct called system thinking is offered as an alternative conceptual framework to restore trust between police and communities. System thinking view the police and community as interdependent parts of a harmonious whole. It focuses on unification based on mutual respect, addressing mutual needs, and co-ownership of problems and solutions. As a process, system thinking examines how our mental models (view of the world) influences our decision making. This training manual represents the start of a new journey. We humbly recognize that policing is more than a career, it is a "calling". It is with this recognition that we offer a systems thinking conceptual framework to repair the breech that currently exists between the police and the community they serve. Melanye V. Smith, PhD

Table of Content

Table of Contents

"LEADERSHIP"

DETERMINES THE CLIMATE FOR POLICE BEHAVIOR

Source: International Association of Police Chiefs

Executive Summary

One of the contradictions of modern day policing is the police code of silence. This phenomenon challenges the role of effective police leadership because it begs the question as to whether police leaders shape the police culture or does the culture shape the leader. In the wake of the latest police shooting in Ferguson, the police culture again comes under fire because of practices such as the code of silence and the "We" versus "Them" mentality. While these practices exist, policies are seldom cited to address them. From the public's view, the absence of official policies questions their expectations of truthfulness, transparency, honesty, and accountability of police leaders and their operations. As a form of organizational learning and behavior, silence, rationalizations, and cover ups can be a defense mechanism used when things go wrong, accidently or otherwise. The We" versus "Them"mentality has been associated with the police code of silence. However, some researchers theorize that this mentality grew out of the internal group conflicts that characterize most police departments and was carried over to the community. An example of intergroup conflict(s) were affirmative action programs.

Unfortunately, this mindset implies that the police are bias toward some members of the communities that they serve. If these claims are true, police are placed in a precarious position with respect to the perception of their ability to enforce the law in an impartial manner. It is a position that conflicts with democratic policing and results in mistrust. In fairness to all police, trust is difficult to built when the police are confronted with dangerous situations daily. This training acknowledges that fear is part of the police culture and that fear reduces trust. The goal of the training is to develop dialogues so that the police and communities can find ways to restore trust.

Dissertation Research

Based on my dissertation, "A Leadership Perspective on the Code of Silence, Procedural Justice, and Police Community Relations", one of the most significant findings was that police behavior was influenced by a culture of fear. As a small qualitative study designed in a social constructionist framework, the study does not claim to try to generalize its finding to a general population but to enhance our understanding of a little known phenomenon. In reference to generalization, Crane (2004) stated that police culture in general has commonalities because of task uniformity and because the task is performed before a similar audience. In the above study, ten retired police chiefs or police executives were interviewed to answer the research question: What is the leadership perspectives on the code of silence, procedural justice, and police community relations? The purpose of the study was to improve our understanding of this "taboo" police practice and solicit suggestions on how to neutralize it.

Methodology

As a phenomenon shrouded in secrecy, an exploratory research design using grounded theory methods was deemed appropriate. The researcher used simultaneous data collected and analysis in conjunction with a three tier coding process. The coding process begin with examining each line of participant's transcript for key concepts. Next, key phrases were examined for similar and dissimilar themes. Finally, the themes were examined for theoretical concepts found in the research literature.

Findings

Based on the above research, the findings revealed that fear was the primary factor that influenced officers, managers, leaders and citizens to behave a certain way. In most fear related situations, participants described a lack of trust. In the above research, participants described fear as a factor associated with the code of silence. Because police culture is stereotypically viewed as macho, any claims that imply police manifest signs of fear in carrying out their job is usually dismissed due to impression management or legal reasons. Unfortunately, deferred maintenance of a problem doesn't mean its going away. It means that it will eventually get worst.

In the code of silence literature, loyalty and social bonding are often cited as plausible explanations why officers participate in cover ups. According to my study, the following fears were mentioned: (a) fear of making a mistake, (b) fear of withdrawal of field support, (c) fear of management inconsistencies, unfair treatment, and disciplinary consequences, (d) fear of retaliation for reporting misconduct, (e) fear of being labeled a snitch, (f) fear of no department protection, (g) fear of being denied transfers, undeniable transfers, and promotions, (h) fear of being terminated, (i) fear of lawsuits, (j) fear of damaging leader's career, and (k) fear of scandal.

The relationship between fear and a lack of trust is exemplified through Covey's research on organizational trust, Covey (2006) suggested a list of organizational behaviors that contribute to a lack of trust. These behaviors included: 1) people manipulate or distort facts, 2) people withhold and hoard information (code of silence), 3) getting the credit is very important, 4) people spin the truth, 5) new ideas are openly resisted and stifled, 6) most people are involved in the blame game, 7) there are many "undiscussables", 8) there are a lot of violated expectations, for which people try to make excuses for, 9) people pretend bad things aren't happening or are in denial, and 10) people often feel unproductive tension –sometimes even fear. The following section identifies some police scandals and the need for police reform. These examples offer the reader an insight into the patterns of police misconduct.

I. Need for Police Community Reform

Past efforts at implementing police community relations program have not been completely successful. From a program perspective, one reason for their failure has been that police community programs have been isolated from the rest of police operations. And from a theoretical and operational perspective, the deterrent model has reached a point of diminishing returns. Yet, no alternative models have been tried. For these reasons, a systems approach is advocated to complement the deterrent model.

The term "Police Community Reform" implies that both the community and the police are part of a broader system. One can not approach one component of the problem and ignore the other and realistically expect success. This call for police community reforms is driven by the need to address the "We" versus "Them" mentality in law enforcement. Changing this philosophy can not be achieved without focusing on managing relationships.

The following section illustrates some of the on going problems within police departments across the country at different times. These incidents could easily be dismissed as "deficiencies associated with a few rogue officers". As a veteran law enforcement officer, I challenge that assessment. Many criminal justice theorist also have challenged that explanation and suggest that the barrel that these individuals come from needs to be examined. When police are recruited, they are socialized into a police culture that already exist. The job of changing the culture is the responsibility of the police chief. When police excutives fail to change their culture, the culture repeats itself. The traditional approach taken by police executives to correct misconduct is to focus on job recruitment and selection. This approach has not worked. The following incidents show the systemic nature of police misconduct and how such misconduct contributes to citizen's mistrust and contributes to a negative emotional perspective of the police.

Reform Needed Due to Corrupt Cops:

Charles Becker – 1915

Charles Becker was a New York City vice cop who ruled the streets from 1890 to 1915, extorting massive amounts of cash from brothels and other illegal businesses in exchange for police protection. His scams went so under the radar that the NYPD even put him on the board that investigated other corrupt cops.

New Orleans – 1994

If you've ever been to "The Big Easy," you know that outside of the tourist area, it can be a lawless terrorland overflowing with corruption. In the 1990s, New Orleans cops had the lowest salaries in the United States, so it's no wonder that they turned to other means to fill their pockets. In 1994, a group of nine officers led by Len Davis were busted in a drug sting, but it was already too late for a woman named Kim Groves. Groves had filed a brutality complaint against Davis. Davis retaliated by having Kim Groves murdered.

The beating of Abner Louima -1997

In 1997 several police officers were called to a popular nightclub in Brooklyn due to a fight, in which a scuffle between bystanders and police erupted. Officer Justin Volpe, was struck by a punch and named Abner Louima as his attacker. After arresting Louima, he was taken to the police station, where Volpe beat, sexually assaulted and sodomized him with a broken broomstick in the bathroom. Volpe had identified the wrong guy and Louima spent 2 months in the hospital recovering from his injuries. Volpe and several other officers were arrested for being involved or attempting to cover up the assaults. In the end, Volpe was sentenced to 30 years in prison and in a subsequent civil suit, Louima was awarded $8.75 million- the largest police brutality settlement in New York history.

The Kathryn Johnson shooting-2006

In 2006, police raided a house in a crime and drug ridden neighborhood in Atlanta. 92 year old Kathryn Johnston, who was home at the time, was startled by the forced invasion and shot once at police officers, not hitting anyone. Officers retaliated and fired 39 shots, hitting Johnson at least 5 times. After searching the home and not finding drugs, the officers planted drugs in the home and convinced a drug informant of theirs to lie to police and tell them that he had bought drugs at Johnson's home earlier that day. It was later determined that they had the wrong address on the warrant and the police officers involved were charged with making false statements, violating oaths of public officers, false imprisonment, and conspiracy to violate rights in result of death.

Chicago bar attack -2007

In 2007, this attack skyrocketed to attention everywhere when a video released showed a 250 pound male Chicago police officer repeatedly kicking and punching a 125 pound female bartender. The bartender, Karolina Obrycka refused to serve intoxicated off-duty police officer Anthony Abbate any more alcohol. The tape, caught on video surveillance from the bar, then shows Abbate confronting Obrycka behind the bar, and Obrycka asking him several times to leave. Abbate then threw her to the floor and kicked and punched her several times. Abbate was arrested and pled not guilty to the 15 charges against him and was only convicted on aggravated battery, he avoided jail time, received a 2 year probation sentence, and was fired from the Chicago Police Department.

Source: Ten Police Scandals By K.Thor Jensen, June 19, 2012.

Reform Needed Due to Failure to Comply with Existing Policies:

In 2012, the Human Rights Watch urged Attorney General Holder to take the following steps at the federal level:

Push for improvements in the federal collection of data on the use of excessive force by federal, state, local, and tribal law enforcement. Federal law (42 USC 14142) requires the US attorney general to collect data on the use of excessive force by law enforcement officers but does not require state, local, and tribal law enforcement to submit any information to the US government on excessive force incidents. The Justice Department has not collected – or has not been able to collect – that data in any useful way. Holder should work with Congress to give incentives to state and local authorities to provide data on excessive force incidents.

Press Congress to pass the End Racial Profiling Act. The End Racial Profiling Act, which had been co-sponsored by President Barack Obama when he was a US senator, is pending before the US Congress. It would condition federal funding in part on certification by local law enforcement agencies that their members had been trained to eliminate practices that result in or encourage racial profiling. Training to eliminate racial profiling may help local law enforcement officials recognize bias and how it can affect their policing decisions and interactions with community members.

Reform Needed to Clarify Existing Programs:

With respect to Stop-and-Frisk in New York City, nearly 700, 000 New Yorkers were detained by police. The program resulted in Judge Shira Scheindlin of Federal District Court granting a class action status to a lawsuit accusing the Police Department of using race as the basis for stopping and frisking New Yorkers. The judge rebuked the city for its "deeply troubling apathy toward New Yorkers' most fundamental constitutional rights," and found "overwhelming evidence" that the program had led to thousands of baseless, unlawful stops. Despite the police claims that the stops keep criminals and weapons off the streets, only about 6 percent of stops lead to arrests, and last year, only one in every 879 stops turned up a gun.

Source: Published: New York Times. EDITORIAL, August 8, 2012 Stop and Frisk in New York City

---

Reform Needed to Fight Change:

On Thursday, May 29, 2014 wrote: The U.S. attorney representing Western Washington on Thursday derided the lawsuit more than 100 Seattle police officers filed in protest of the new federally mandated use-of-force policies. Meanwhile, the Seattle Police Department issued its own brief statement distancing itself from the claims of the plaintiffs.

The federal lawsuit filed Wednesday -- signed by about 9 percent of all police officers on Seattle's force -- claims that the new use-of-force policies to be enacted this year are too complicated and put police officers and the public at greater danger. The suit also argues that the new policies violate officers' constitutional rights to defend themselves and conduct reasonable searches to investigate criminal activity.

A 2011 report from the U.S. Department of Justice derided the Seattle Police Department for a "pattern of excessive force" and evidence of possible racially biased policing.

After that, the city came to an agreement with the feds to enact a series of reforms intended to address the problems named in the report.

"We are making significant and positive progress in the reform of the Seattle Police Department," Durkan said Thursday, adding that a minority of officers were found to have practiced "unconstitutional policing."

Though the lawsuit complained that the new guidelines are out of touch with real street policing, Durkan disputed that claim, saying the rules were written by police and for police with input welcome at every stage.

The department passed drafts of new policies to the Justice Department, which then approved them.

Durkan said that the reform process will be undeterred by Wednesday's lawsuit.

"Reform is underway," she said. "Get on the train or leave."

Seattle Police Department spokeswoman Renee Witt said Thursday afternoon the agency doesn't comment on active lawsuits, but the media relations department put out a statement addressing the matter soon afterward.

"This lawsuit ... does not represent the views of the Seattle Police Department," the statement said. "SPD will continue working with the Department of Justice, elected representatives and community members to ensure our officers have the tools, training and personnel needed to provide effective, constitutional and lawful public safety services to our city." (Burton, L, 2014) *at lynsiburton@seattlepi.com.*

Reform Needed to Urge Implementations of Existing Recommendations:

Based om the Charlotte-Mecklenburg Police Department, a framework for institutionalizing police reform identified 13 lessons recommended by Ikerd and Walker (2010). Out of the 13 recommendations, four are listed.

Recommendation 1: A department must address the Organizational Culture.

Recommendation 3: Develop recruiting procedures to target officers who have the skills conducive to problem-oriented policing and community policing.

Recommendation 4: Develop a training curriculum focusing on the elements of the new program.

Recommendation 5: Include elements of a police reform in the promotions process, performance evaluations, and rewards Systems (Ikerd & Walker, 2010).

The above events indicate that patterns of misconduct exist across the country. There is also evidence that police executives have proposed recommendations in some cases to address departmental problems. In other instances, some of these same issues have been addressed by different blue ribbon commissions at different time periods in policing history. In other words, there is an abundance of literature and recommendations throughout policing history which identifies and/or suggest solutions to some of these reoccurring problems. This author believes that the reasons these problems continue is because managers focus on behavioral outcomes and use the deficit model to explain misconduct. By shifting the blame for the problem on the individual, police executives fail to examine the context and the overall process that contributes to the behavior. This point is very significant because if police executives use the deficit model to blame officers when something goes wrong; then, the same thinking is used to explain their actions towards citizens (suspects) when something goes wrong also. A further point that needs to be mentioned is that the deficit model exonerates the police of any accountability issues. Is it possible that the police do contribute to the relationships with the communities they serve? If so, how can they improve their relationships with the community?

With respect to the "We" versus "Them" mentality, it is part of police cultural DNA. As such, it represents how police view their job and the world around them. Unfortunately, this mentality reflects properties of the deficit model and perpetuates a cycle of non-accountability with respect to some police decision making. This author believes that system thinking can be applied to paradoxes such as the "We" versus "Them" mentality in an effort to find areas of mutual needs and mutual cooperation. The next section is an overview of system thinking approach to police community relations.

II. System Thinking

As part of developing a systems approach to police community reform, this section introduces a learning organization framework that includes system thinking. The term learning organization should not be confused with organizational learning. A learning organization is one which continuously redefines its goals and vision through continuous learning. In contrast, organizational learning is the outcome of what is learned (good or bad). Senge (1990) used system thinking as one of five components associated with a learning organization. The other four components are personal mastery, mental models, shared vision, and team building. System thinking was defined as viewing the organization as a whole rather than the summation of its individual parts. In terms of police community relations, system thinking incorporates the community as a co-partner in developing policies aimed at improving problematic issues and building trust.

In my dissertation on the code of silence, the findings implied that code of silence related behavior was influenced by a "We" versus "Them" mentality that police were socialized to. While there is a consensus in law enforcement that this mentality is detrimental to police community relations, there has been little success in changing it. At present, it contradicts most values that support police community relations. For police executives, it is the most challenging paradox that exist in law enforcement today. This mentality becomes part of a default culture in policing when leaders fail to address it. If ignored, it fosters role ambiguity, promotes division and distrust, justifies a win-lose scenario in most police actions, and perpetuates fear among police and community members. How do we address the systemic problems that face law enforcement when meaningful community feedback is not solicited nor measured? Today, police leaders are confronted with problems that are quite different from those decades ago.

Immigration, terrorist, technology, politics, crime, order maintenance, budgets shortages, and community dissatisfaction are problems that are complex, dynamic, and with constant uncertainty.

The perspective held by most law enforcement personnel is that crime is influenced by unemployment, poor education, poverty, single parent homes, etc. In a sense of fairness, these social problems can't be solved by the police alone. They are systemic in nature, just as police patterns of misconduct, police don't have any control over these factors but they should have control over how they management their behave. The same holds true for citizens. They should have control over how they behave. In terms of how police think about crime, it can be defined as linear. Police view their role as independent of the other variables that influence crime. This one directional cause and effect form of thinking reflects linear thinking rather than system thinking. For example, take our current criminal justice deterrent model that was based on the assumption that if we arrest criminals; then, it will deter them from engaging in future criminal behavior. While the police are successful in making arrest, the Bureau of Justice Statistics (2005), reported that within three years of release, parolees are rearrested by 67 % percent; and, within five years , the percentage increases to 76.6 % percent of prisoners re-arrested. So from an holistic view, police success may be limited in terms of how well the overall system works. These numbers reflect that the deterrent model needs to be reconceptualized. System thinking suggest that police and citizen relationships are non-linear, interdependent, and interactions have to be constantly managed for integration.

One trend of thought is that because so much is invested in the deterrent model that no one wants to change it or admit that the system has problems. Gharajedaghi (2006) added that no one wants to tell you that your recipe for success is now ineffective. Argyris (1980) noted that individuals use defense mechanisms to block new ideas and problems that may be embarrassing to discuss. Failing to addressing "taboo" issues such as the "We" versus "Them" mentality only makes the problem worse. Ouinn (1996) stated that when problems are not addressed; then, people revert back to their old way of thinking and behaving. This is why Schein (2004) stated that either a leader will shape the culture or the culture will shape the leader.

In a system thinking scenario, the assumptions associated with the "We" versus "Them" mentality would be examined. This mentality may be held by some police and by some community members. One fundamental characteristic of system thinking is that it is concern with answering "why" something occurs rather than just what happen. In terms of answering the "why" question regarding patterns of police misconduct and patterns of social ills in some communities, system thinking can be used to better understand what correlations exist and what suitable solutions can be jointly proposed. System thinking can be used to examine the learning process of faulty thinking and errant behavior that contribute to these patterns. The relevance of the "We" versus "Them" mentality is that it is part of police culture and therefore it may be acknowledge in order for effective solutions to be posed. Officers become socialized to this mentality when they become part of the police culture.

From a practical standpoint, every situation that a police officer encounters is not viewed the same and every police officer doesn't see similar situations the same. This is part of the complexity, dynamics, and uncertainty of the job. Despite the individual differences , the police culurture has a strong influence in socializing all police into the "We" versus "Them" mentality. This training provides an opportunity to address this mentality in community forums.

Despite the absence of these kinds of police community dialogues, police are judged as breaching the psychological trust contract when something goes wrong in the course of their duties. Because police leadership has not addressed this mentality, citizens perceive that the police adopt this mentality in every situation. However, most cops understand that this mentality exist when fighting cartels, terrorist, and season criminals but not ordinary citizens. Unfortunately, problem(s) arises when this mind set is applied in the form of deadly force when handcupped suspects or unarmed suspects are alleged to have a weapon. When the police can't distinguish between situations when they can preserve life versus situations where they must take a life; then, the public loses confidence in them and their training. As mentioned, the absence of a policy on the "We" versus "Them" mentality contributes to issues related to policy clarification and police role ambiguities. In addition, the absence of written policies on this topic may contribute to the following negative outcomes: (1) the community perceives that the police as bias in performing their jobs, (2) the "We" versus "Them" mentality will continue to promote fear rather than trust, and (3) the mentality will erroneously be used as a mechanism for police solidarity rather than a shared vision which unifies police and community.

System thinking provides both citizens and police the opportunity to replace a win-lose mentality with a win-win mentality. In comparing system thinkings to traditional linear thinking, Gharajedaghi (2006), characterized the former as: a) frames problems based on longevity patterns of behavior rather than isolated incidents b) places responsibility on the internal policy maker and overseer of the organization for inefficiencies rather than blaming external factors, c) emphacizes pattern recognition as having a greater weight than just focusing on details, d) focuses on learning the assumptions that drive the behavior instead of listing factors that influence the behavior, e) understanding that causes and effect(s) are multi-directional and influence each other, f) and that all models, theories and/or assumptions are temporary not permanent. One other important aspect of system thinking is that it is concern with continuous improvement of a never ending process.

Law enforcement is such a process. The training in this manual can be used by police, managers, leaders, citizens, victims, and even suspects. By approaching crime reduction and community relationships from the supply side, the training can address an individual's self – esteem and self – portrait issue(s) that may result in negative thinking and negative behavior. If the self-awareness and development training can be taught to at risk youths before they become entangled in the criminal system; then, the police and community will see a decrease in the number of arrest and confrontations. System thinking recognizes both the interdependency of both the police and the community and their mutual concern for building trust. The following section identifies the ten common principles associated with community policing.

III. Ten Principles of Community Policing

Change   Equity

Leadership   **Trust**

Vision   Empowerment

Partnership   Service

Problem Solving   Accountability

Source: International Association of Police Chieefs.

In the above section, each of the ten community policing principles contribute to implementing a successful police community relations. However, the glue that holds all the other principles together is **TRUST**. By definition, trust involves the risk of making one's self vulnerable based on the expectation that the other person will act in your best interest. For example, we trust leaders. We trust police because of the role they symbolize. We trust people licensed by professions because of the accreditation standards of that institution. We live in a society where we have to cooperate with one another to get something accomplished so we learn that we have to trust some people. When someone fails to live up to our expectations, we lose trust in that person or institution.

Due to some of the negative behavior that police have engaged in, our perception of the police is that they are not trustworthy. Law enforcement must continue to explore ways to improve the trust between themselves and the citizens they serve. To this extent, the training in this manual seeks to enhance our trust building capacities by elevating our awareness thru the material presented. The next section identifies some of the existing best practices for internal and external strategies to improve police community trust relations.

IV. Best Practices for Community Trust-Building

Internal Strategies

Institute culture-changing policies, programs, and training to solidify the department's core values and ethical principles.

Consider developing an Office of Professional Standards to manage these activities.

Develop a comprehensive recruiting plan; recruit and hire people with a service orientation.

Provide continuous training in ethics, integrity, and discretion to every officer from the time he or she enters the police academy through the time of retirement.

Conduct consistent evaluations and review of all employees, and immediately address negative behavior and reward positive behavior.

Use some form of Early Intervention System, not only in Internal Affairs, but to prevent behavior that may lead to an Internal Affairs complaint and investigation.

External Strategies

Institute some form of community oriented policing program to better engage the community.

Develop a citizen's police academy.

Use the media to publicize positive programs and stories about the department.

Hold workshops on subjects of interest to the community.

Conduct a community survey to gauge and enhance public perception.

Proactively involve the public.

Source: Office of Community Oriented Police Services (2007)

V. Training Overview

Among the components of community policing cited by the International Association of Police Chiefs, none are of greater importance than trust. The following section delineates a holistic training process that will supplement existing internal and external community trust building strategies. The premise of the training is based on the belief that when we reduce fear; then, we increase trust. Over the course of this training, participants will be exposed to educational material on toxic thoughts, mental models, transactional analysis, emotional intelligence, almygdala hijack, internal value principles, procedural justice strategies, dispute resolution, and cooperative learning. The training consist of both pedagogical and role playing. The pedagogical aspect of the training consist of material for knowledge acquisition and comprehension. The training will utilize a problem solving format in order to allow the participants the opportunity to apply what they have learned.

While the initial purpose of the training was to focus on improving trust between police and the communities which they serve, system thinking requires behavior to be understood within the culturual context. The training had to be re-conceptualized in order to address the "We" versus "Them" mentality which is part of the police cultural DNA. At present, while this mentality conflicts with the philosophy and values associated with police community relations,

it formally has been ignored as a legitimate concern. Because these are conflicting values, one of the objectives of the training is to explore ways where these seemingly opposing views, beliefs, and values can complement each other. This training will enhance the self awareness of all particpants and help individuals identify their own personal biases which can contribute to poor decisions and problem solving. System thinking attempts to examine the assumptions associated with our behavior and how our experiences influence these assumptions. In essence, it examines the "why" of our thinking.

This researcher believes past efforts to build trust between the police and citizens have failed because the "We" versus "Them" mentality was not incorporated into the training. As I have depicted in the police cultural iceberg, we as individuals, same as organizations, have experiences that are more conscious than others. Some scientist say that we are conscious of 10 percent of what we know and the other 90 percent of what we experience is stored in the unconscious mind. With respect to the organization language, the "We" versus "Them" mentality represents what we refer to as theories in use. Theories in use are the norms of behavior that are not written down as department policies or procedures.

As illustrated by the cultural iceberg, the theories in use concerns are found below the water line. They are topics that no one wants to talk about due to fear of retaliation. The "We" versus "Them" mindset falls in this category. However, before there can be meaningful police community relations and trust building, police organizations or police leaders must address this paradox. Most police professionals or practitioners acknowledge its existence; yet, it would be an aberration if a department formulated a policy or mission statement addressing it. The absence of a policy addressing this "We" versus "Them" mentality, is similar to the lack of a policy on the code of silence. The absence of a policy implies that the "We" versus "Them" mentality doesn't exist. This incongruence between existence and non-existence of this mentality creates an integrity problem for police organizations. And as a consequence of ignoring these aspects of police culture, problem solving is ineffective coupled with the fact that the public feels that they can't trust the police. The irony of this whole situation is that the police, by their own actions of ignoring cultural taboos have contributed to this lost of trust. This training along with system thinking is designed to address these kinds of issues. Below is an illustration of the cultural iceberg.

Cultural Iceberg

Historically, another reason cited as to why police community relations has failed is because some departments viewed police community relations as a public relation prank. In order to overcome this assumptions, police administrator have to do more than "say the right things, they must do the right things".   Behavioral training cannot be isolated from the context in which it occurs in order for the police culture to change. The cultural iceberg represents a visual topography of the existing police landscape which includes both cultural assumptions that we are aware of and assumptions that we are sometimes unaware of. This discrepancy between what is known and unknown contributes to misalignments and integration issues between "What we say" versus "What we do".   These paradoxes, incongruences, contradictions and conflicting values are items requiring discussion, understanding, and balance. System thinking offers a suitable approach to addressing these problematic issues.

Community Policing (Overt Principles)

Trust Building, Partnership, Transparency, Fair Treatment, Respect, Input, Participation

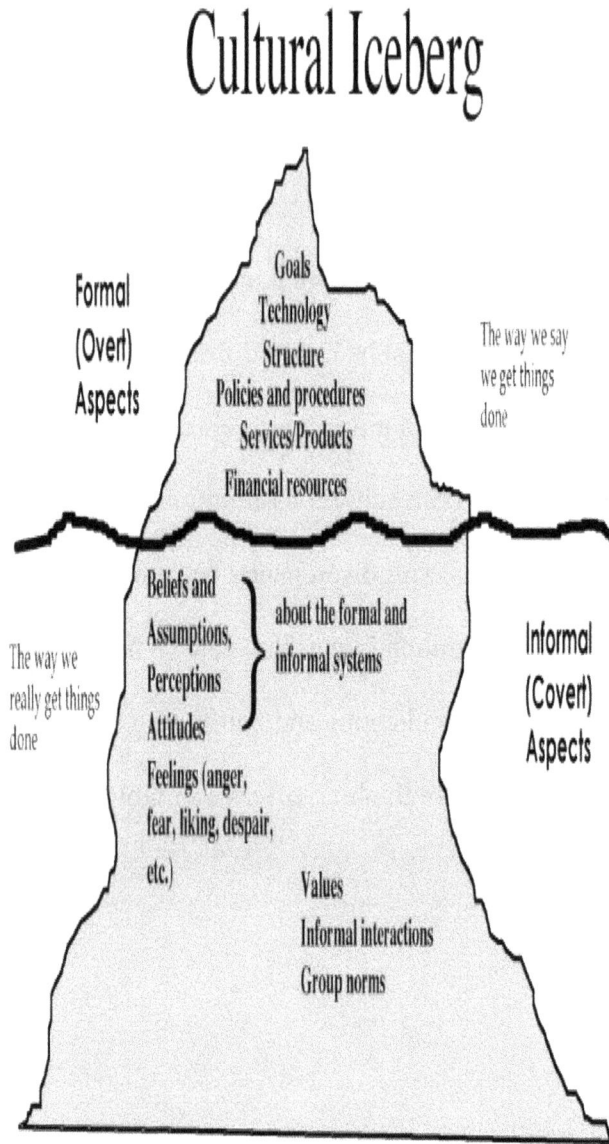

Cultural Iceberg

Formal (Overt) Aspects

The way we say we get things done

Goals
Technology
Structure
Policies and procedures
Services/Products
Financial resources

The way we really get things done

Beliefs and Assumptions, Perceptions Attitudes Feelings (anger, fear, liking, despair, etc.)

about the formal and informal systems

Informal (Covert) Aspects

Values
Informal interactions
Group norms

Created by Stanley N. Herman, TRW Systems Group, 1970

"We" versus "Them" (Covert Practices of Police Culture)

Police Code of Silence, Negative Peer Pressure, Toxic Thoughts, Trust Eroding, Health Issues

Misconduct, In-Group Fighting, Weak Leadership, Fear, Retaliation, Cover-ups, Secrecy

Training Goals and Assumptions

The goal of the training is to enhance awareness and to improve the organization's trust building capacity among police and citizens. In order to accomplish this, the following assumptions have been identified:

O Assumption One – Building trust is the antidote to overcome fear.

O Assumption Two – Integrity is expected by all stakeholders.

O Assumption Three – Police and citizens will engage in open dialogue, conduct fair procedures, practice fair treatment, practice mutual respect, and be honest.

O Assumption Four – Individuals must master components of personal trust before they are effective in creating organizational trust.

O Assumption Five – Police Administrators will communicate through policy formulation and organizational practices to the rank and file that the "We" versus "Them" undermines trust building with the community.

O Assumptive Six-Individuals value continuous self improvement and learning.

Training Objectives

By participating in this training, participants should improve their awareness and self-efficacy in the following areas:

1) Participants should improve their interpersonal communication and social skills.
2) Participants should understand how the brain works during extreme stress.
3) Participants should be able to use trust building strategies within the community.
4) Participants should understand the other person's perspective (empathy).
5) Participants should understand how to control their emotions.
6) Participants should understand their emotional history.
7) Participants should understand that toxic thoughts harm their health.
8) Participants should understand positive thoughts reduce stress.
9) Participants should learn to treat people fairly and apply rules consistently.
10) Participants should understand that they must master their personal trust before they can create positive organizational trust.
11) Participants should learn that listening first is important.
12) Participants should learn that treating people with respect is the "best" ice breaker.
13) Participants should understand that their prejudices have been learned; therefore, they can be unlearned.
14) Participants should understand that the brain stores and recalls events and emotions.
15) Participants should understand the 12 internal change principles.
16) Participants should understand the relationship between "amygdala hijacking" and fear.
17) Participants should understand the concepts of "mental models and system thinking".

Description

In commencing the workshop, the instructor will pass out and have the class or community group complete a trust questionnaire. The instructor will tell them to just hold on to it after completion. Next, the instructor will ask for three teams consisting of three individuals to volunteer for a role play exercise or he will draft them. Once the teams are selected, officers, management, and/or citizens will select from the range of situational fear taxonomies associated with the code of silence research study. Ideally, if time permits, participants should alternate roles.

The typology included (a) fear of making a mistake, (b) fear of withdrawal of field support, (c) fear of management inconsistencies, unfair treatment, and disciplinary consequences,

(d) fear of retaliation for reporting misconduct, (e) fear of being labeled a snitch, (f) fear of no department protection, (g) fear of being denied transfers, undeniable transfers, and promotions, (h) fear of being terminated, (i) fear of lawsuits, (j) fear of damaging leader's career (k) fear of scandal, (l) fear of inaccurate report, and (m) fear of investigative cover-up.

In each skit, there will be a third individual whose role will be that of the agitator symbolizing "negative peer pressure". The objective of the exercise is for participants to address and solve a trust problem from the above fear taxonomy. For instance, if participants chose the fear of making a mistake; then, they will take three minutes to create a problem situation that needs to be resolved. One of the participants will be asked a task to do toward solving the problem Since this is a before and after training module, participants will meet for the second time after the training and apply what they learned. The purpose of the task assignment is to create a trust contract between parties.based on mutual expectations. During the initial training exercise, the audience will take down notes on a separate sheet of paper identifying what types of trust building or trust eroding behaviors that they observed.

Once all teams have performed their skits and the participants jotted down their observations, the next phase of training will consist of the instructor presenting educational information to the group to enhance their awareness about fear and building trust. After this material is presented, the third phase of the training will consist of the instructor distributing a trust performance checklist for the class to complete. The class and/or community group will grade each participant except the agitator. The rationale for not grading the agitator was because he or she was used to represented a contextual aspect of the problem (peer pressure).

Overall Procedures

After three teams perform a six to seven minute role playing skit based on the fear typology, the instructor will present relevant education material, types of interventions, and strategies that enhance trust building. At the conclusion of the presentation, the trainer will request the same three teams to return to present their final role playing skit and to demonstrate what they learned from the material gleaned. After the final skit, the trainer will provide the group with the trust performance checklist to evaluate participants' performance. Upon completion of the performance checklist, the group will discuss their assessment of the participants' performance. If time allows, the group will use the trust performance checklist to evaluate themselves based on their answers to the trust questionnaire. When performing this training for a department, the instructor will retain evaluations if requested.

Conclusion

Overrall, this training is a holistic approach to self-awareness, interpersonal skills, and enhancing one's capacity to build trust. The training will focus on how negative experiences influence our view of the world and how we have to change our thought process in order to change our life. Within law enforcement, the "We" versus "Them" mentality is one type of cultural outlook that has negative connotations which undermine trust building. This training tries to get participants to question their own biases, values, beliefs, assumptions, and behavior as a clue in how they relate to others. And if there are discrepancies between what we say and what we do; then, the training can be used to close the gap. The next section will highlight a conceptual framework of the training for building trust between the police and the community:

Figure 1:   Building a Cycle of Trust:

VI. Building a Cycle of Trust (System Thinking)

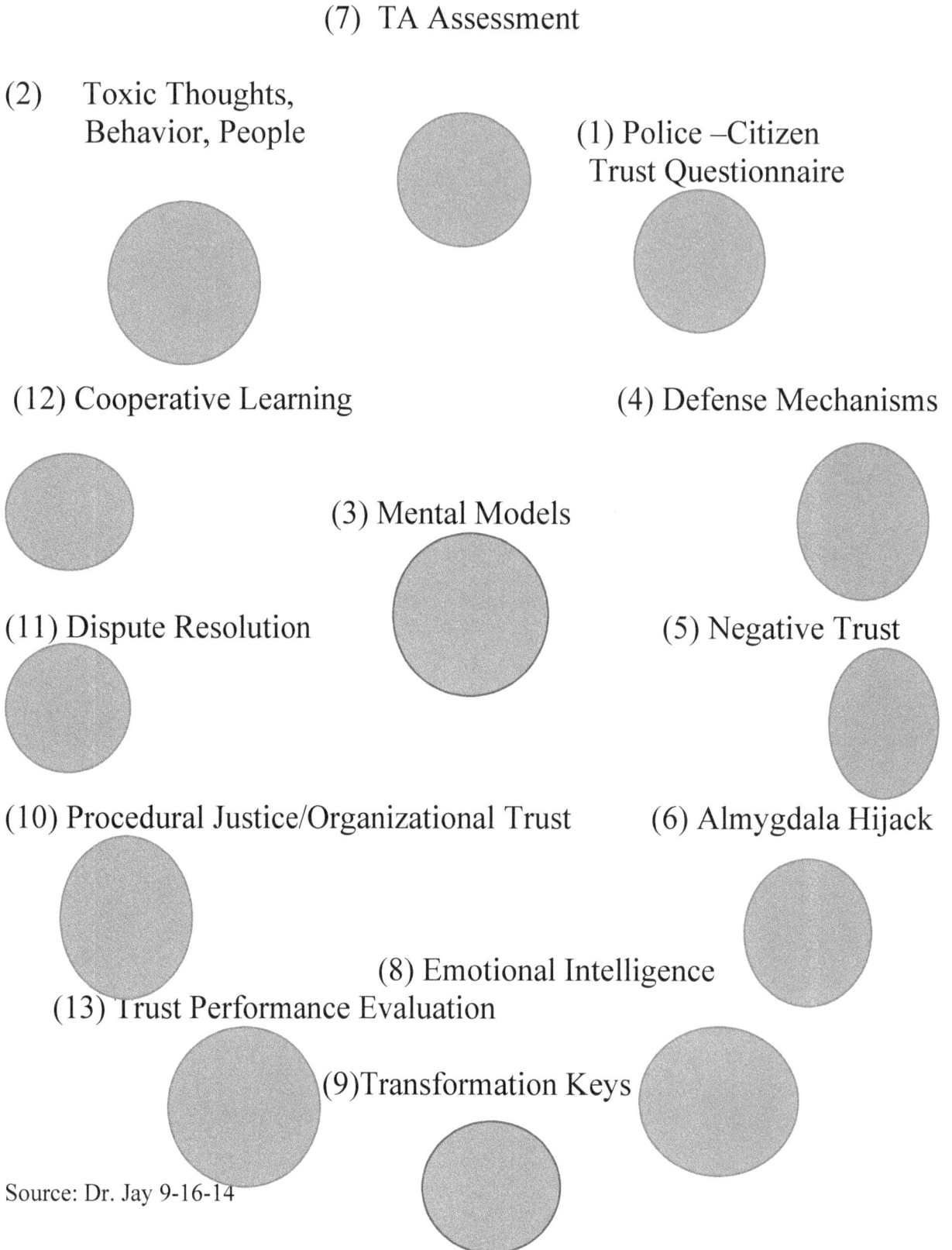

(7) TA Assessment

(2) Toxic Thoughts,
Behavior, People

(1) Police –Citizen
Trust Questionnaire

(12) Cooperative Learning

(4) Defense Mechanisms

(3) Mental Models

(11) Dispute Resolution

(5) Negative Trust

(10) Procedural Justice/Organizational Trust

(6) Almygdala Hijack

(8) Emotional Intelligence

(13) Trust Performance Evaluation

(9)Transformation Keys

Source: Dr. Jay 9-16-14

VII. Police – Community Trust Questionnaire

1. *I have negative emotions about trusting* _____*(affirmation)*__
   *Comment:*_____

2. *The reason it's hard for me to trust is because*_____
   Comment: _____

3. *I believe people don't trust othe people because* _____
   Comment: _____

4. *I can describe a story where there was a breach of trust* _____
   Comment: _____

5. *Since that breach of trust, have you tried to rebuild trust with that person How*_____
   Comment: _____

6. *I don't trust some family members (immediate) Why*_____
   Comment: _____

7. *I don't trust people in different races Why*_____*(cultural bias)*
   Comment: _____

8. *I don't trust some of my co-workers Why*_____
   Comment: _____

9. *I don't trust my boss Why*_____
   Comment: _____

10. *I don't trust some police officers Why*_____
    Comment: _____

11. *I don't trust some citizens_Why*_____
    Comment: _____

12. *One person that I do trust is Why*_____
    Comment: _____

13. *Another person that I do trust is __Why*_____
    Comment: _____

14. *What trait is most important to you in developing a trusting relationship*_____
    Comment: _____

15. What would you be willing to do to rebuild the lost trust of someone _____

    Comment: _____

16. What obstacle keeps you from learning how to trust again _____

    Comment: _____

Dr. Jay Hall (9-16-14)

VIII. Negative Trust Behaviors

In studying the code of silence, participants shared various incidents where fear or the perception of fear motivated individuals to cover up facts or engage in false reporting. In most situations, fear was a manifestation of the absence of trust. The decision not to trust someone and to trust someone is a learned behavior. Part of the training in this manual will attempt to help workshop participants examine their assumptions and reasoning for trusting or not-trusting individuals that they interact with. Before, presenting material on this topic, Covey (2006) layed the foundation for organizational trust by discussing the components of personal trust. Covey stated that individuals have four components of personal trust. These component are: integrity, motive, capacity, and results. One of the assumptions of this training is that individuals should mastered their personal trust components before being given the responsibility of creating a climate of trust within their organization. Integrity is the most important component with respect to personal trust. If there is a gap between what you say and do, your integrity is on the line.

Covey defined integrity as the absence of a gap between one's motives and one's actions. This definition can also be applied to the behavior of organizations. When an organization's espouse theories (official policies) differ from their theories in use (informal practices); then, a discrepancy exist. Therefore, an organization can suffer from character flaws just like individuals. The following section identifies some of the negative behavior(s) associated with a low trust organization and is repeated for reinforcement.

Characteristics of Low Trust Organizations

In terms of an organization, Covey (2006) identified the following negative characteristics of low trust organizations: 1) people manipulate or distort facts, 2) people withhold and hoard information (code of silence), 3) getting the credit is very important, 4) people spin the truth, 5) new ideas are openly resisted and stifled, 6) most people are involved in the blame game, 7) there are many "undiscussables", 8) there are a lot of violated expectations, for which people try to make excuses for, 9) people pretend bad things aren't happening when they are and 10) people often feel unproductive tension –sometimes even fear. Without drawing a direct parallel, some of the above characteristics match descriptions of police culture that include secrecy, fear, taboos, code of silence, cynicism, manipulation and deception.

In addition to Covey, Fraser (2010) also identified some trust related behaviors. Fraser (2010) conducted a series of interviews with focus groups to determine which factors most frequently contributed to breakdowns in trust. The most commonly mentioned factors included:

☐ Disrespectful behaviors: discounting people or their contributions, disregarding feelings and input, and blaming other people for problems;

☐ Communication issues: not listening to others, not working to understand the other party, and breakdown in communication around major changes;

☐ Unmet expectations: broken promises, breaches in the psychological contract, breach of confidentiality, and breach of rules;

☐ Ineffective leadership: punishing those who challenged authority, poor decisions, favoritism, or unwillingness to address major issues;

☐ Unwillingness to acknowledge: taking no responsibility for mistakes or issues, not owning issues or the violation itself, placing self before the group;

☐ Performance issues: unwilling or unable to perform basic job duties, making mistakes, issues of general competence;

☐ Incongruence: misaligned with or not honoring core values, mission, practices; actions do not match words; and

Structural issues, including changes in systems and procedures, lack of structure or too much structure, and misalignment of job duties and authority (as cited in Kramer & Lewicki, 2010, p. 251).

Instead of describing behavior that breaks down trust, the next section list behaviors

that reduce fear in the work place.

IX. Fear Reducing Behaviors in the Workplace

In the above section, Both Covey (2006) and Frazer (2010) have identified behaviors that undermine trust. In this section, authors, Ryan and Oestreich (1991) will identify behaviors that would reduce fear in the workplace. While the terms of trust and fear can be viewed as two sides of the same coin, law enforcement prefers to frame their concerns using trust building. The only problem with ignoring the fear component is that this approach may fail to answer why people don't trust the police. In my opinion, this failure to discover why people don't trust the police or fear the police omits pertinent information from citizens which may lead to a better understanding of the issue and its resolution. For leaders, the following behaviors for reducing fear are extremely important since they are charged with the responsibility of creating an organization where participation, learning, and feedback are welcome by employees and citizens.

Fear Reducing Behaviors

1. All employees are encouraged to express their ideas and be visible to top leadership.

2. Supervisors and employees admit their mistakes, and both recognize that mistakes are inevitable. With mutual   support, employees and supervisors help each other figure out how to do things differently in the future.

3. In general, information is shared not restricted. There is a mutual understanding of the types of information that need to be restricted.

4. People collaborate on important issues and are asked to give their views. Whenever possible, consensus governs decision-making.

5. Instead of creating "us or them" distinctions, people talk in terms of "we."

6. People focus on big picture issues and avoid endless conflict over details. People agree to reach and abide by consensus so that the organization can move forward.

7. People respect organizational structures and do not use their positions as weapons. When conflict and problems occur, communication increases with the goal of deciding together what is right in a particular situation.

8. Rather than discrediting each other's competence, employees and managers value each other's background and experience. The organization has a strict rule about intentionally discrediting anyone.

9. Concerns, criticisms, and conflicts are openly voiced. Neither employees, nor managers act in ways that would undermine, manipulate or sabotage each other's efforts.

10. Cynicism is not a serious problem because people are encouraged to express their concerns, frustrations, discouragement, confusion, and anger (Ryan and Oestreich, 1991).

Comparing Trust and Fear

In comparing the information provided by Frazer (2010) and Ryan and Oestreich (1991), the authors sought similar outcomes. For example, Frazer stated that behavior undermining trust included: Unwillingness to acknowledge: taking no responsibility for mistakes or issues, not acknowledging problematic issues or violations, and having a personal agenda. In comparison, Ryan and Oestreich suggested behavior for eliminating fear included: Supervisors and employees should admit their mistakes, and both recognize that mistakes are inevitable. Using employee input as another example, Frazer stated that discounting people or their contributions, disregarding feelings and input, and blaming other people for problems are ways to undermine trust.

In a similar vein, Ryan and Oestreich stated that all employees should be encouraged to express their ideas to top leaders. Employee input is a principle relevant to procedural justice which will be addressed later in the manual as a trust building strategy. Essentially, these authors are saying the same thing: one from the perspective of trust and the other from the perspective of fear. Of major significance here and as documented in the literature, Ryan and Oestreich stated that leaders should be careful not to create the "Us" versus "Them" mentality in the workplace. This suggestion sounds familiar in terms of the current discussion on the "We" versus "Them" mentality inherent to police culture.

The relationship between trust and fear is an inverse one. When we increase fear, we reduce trust and vice versa. A very important aspect of the "We" versus "Them" mindset is that it reflects how police think and it implies that police have a predisposition. It is very similar to the self-fulling phophecy where authoritarian figures create the conditions that drive certain behavior and then say I told you so. This is a form of psychological manipulation. When authoritarian figures fail to correct situations and fail to address problematic issues; then, they are in agreement by omission (silence). System thinking is an alternative to the win-lose models. System thinking suggest that it is no longer my problem or your problem, it is our problem.

Negative Trust and Fear Chart

The chart below reflects the trust and fear reseach of Covey (2006), Ryan and Oestreich (1991), and Fraizer (2010) which reflects information on low trust organization, reducing fear in organizations, and behaviors that undermine trust.

Low Trust-Building and Fear Reducing Behaviors:

Covey (2006)	Ryan and Oestreich (1991)	Frazer (2010)
Low Trust:	Fear Reduction:	Undermine Trust:
Manipulating the facts.	Encourage to express ideas.	Disrespectful behaviors.
Withholding information.	Admitting mistakes.	Not listening to others.
Spinning the truth.	Information sharing.	Broken promises.
Ignoring new ideas.	Mutual agreement on restricted	Taking no responsibility
Avoiding undiscussables.	on restricted information.	for mistakes.
Engaging in the blame game.	Engage in collaboration.	Leaders punishing critics
Practicing denial.	Eliminate "We" vs. "Them"	Misalignment of intent
Creating climate of fear.	work environment.	and actions.
	Don't sabotage others work.	

In an effort to create an environment or culture that promotes trust building between the police and the community, the next section describes a process called transactional analysis which can be used to identify where negative emotions and trust issues originated.

X. Transactional Analysis

In this section of the training manual, I will introduce transactional analysis as an intervention tool that assist individuals in developing better self- awareness, personal growth, interpersonal social skills, communication skills, and overall performance. But more important, transactional analysis provides a means of locating the source of toxic thoughts and self-esteem issues. According to Harris (2004), the brain tape records all events and experiences and is capable of retrieving them. In conjunction with the work of Eric Berne, three sources of memory or ego states existed in each person. Essentially, under this theory, our personality consist of three components. The **Parent** component represents the external rules that we were taught growing up and continued through adult life. The **Child** component represents the recording of events as seen from the perspective of a child. These recordings also records the emotions associated with the events that an individual experienced as a child. In some cases, a person make respond to a current events negatively because of a negative incident in their history.

Finally, the **Adult component** represents our critical thinking and our ability to examine the information taught to us by external influences such as our parents, peers, gangs, civic groups, or organization. The adult also examines our childlike emotiions to determine if they are inappropriate for a particular situation. In this sense, the adult is like our real-time computer. The idea role of the adult is to assess, gather facts, mediate and sort out conflicting information. These three components of our personality respond differently based on our experiences.

According to Maslow (1954), human beings have the following hierarchy of needs: physiological, safety, love/belonging, esteem, and self-actualization. Sometimes, when the emotional needs of a child are not meet, an emotion scar is carried from childhood to adulthood.

In many cases, the adult is unaware of the emotional scar which may affect their present or future relationships. As such, our emotional experiences good or bad become part of our emotional history. Events that can shape a child's emotional development are divorces, domestic violence, rape, incest, alcoholism, drug abuse, parental neglect, or parental abuse. Sometimes the emotional scars are so great that we may need professional help to heal them. Based on these negative feelings, an individual is more prone to act bad because they feel bad. Sometimes bad

habits are passed from one generation to the next. This is where the concept of generational curse comes from. However, the good news is that you can break the generations of bad habits and become the first generational blessing.

While transactional analysis has been used in businesses, education, communication, and management, I believe it can be used in police community trust building relations. The source of our socialization starts at home. Our emotional make up is influenced by our family relationships. If we experienced positive feedback, love, and caring; we tend to develop confidence, trust, and a positive self-esteem based on a reliable (dependable) support system. On the other hand, if our family support system is undependable and fails to protect us from physical and psychological harm; then, we tend not to trust people. These levels are some the primal levels identified in Maslow's Hierarchy of Needs. As a result of our experiences as a child (positive or negative), our view of the world is shaped by these experiences. Some experiences are so devastaging that we suppress them for years. Because most negative experiences are personal, we tend to keep these negative thoughts to our selves. This applies to both police and citizens. The cultural iceberg concept can also be applied to our emotional baggage which is often buried below the surface.

TA offers all individuals a method of understanding, processing, and changing negative thoughts that derived from negative experiences. It also provides a means of examining our world view based on what we were taught at home, at school, at our jobs, and in our communities. Sometimes, what we have been taught is bias and TA can help re-examine our prejudices. In addition to, TA also uses several other components. These components are listed below:

SELF – AWARENESS

P- A- C PERSONALITY EGO STATES

FOUR LIFE POSITIONS

LIFE SCRIPTS

TRANSACTIONS

GAMES

STROKING (Harris, 2004)

In addition to tracing our emotional make-up back to our family structures by using the P-A-C components, TA describes four life positions based on the positive or negative relations that a child may have developed at home depending whether the child had a nurturing parent or a neglectful parent.

Harris (2004) identified four life positions that characterized how our personal experiences influence our view of world (mental models). The following four life positions are: 1) I'm Ok, You're OK, 2) I'm Ok, You're Not Ok, 3) I'm Not OK, but You're Ok, and 4) I'm Not OK, and You're Not OK. Based on these life positions, if individual A is OK, and individual B is Ok; then, neither one should have a problem trusting each other. However, if individual A or individual B occupy either of the remaining three life positions such as I' Ok and Your're not Ok; I'm not OK but you're

OK or I'm not OK and You're not Ok; then, the ability not to trust the other person is greatly magnified. Here, this author is making an educated guess that individuals with high esteems are more willing to trust others than individuals with low self-esteems.

Transactional Analysis and the "We" versus "Them" Lifescript

The concept of life scripts is most interesting when we examine the current police mentality. As a life script, the "We" versus "Them" police mentality is similar to the script of I'm Ok but You're not OK. Under this life script, the police are saying to the public: "We" are OK but You're not OK. If there is the slightest modicum of truth to this assertion; then, the implication may mean that the police are operating from an unhealthy organizational script. If so, this training may benefit the organization as a whole; not just, its' individual members. From an individual standpoint, a police officer or a citizen that operates from an unhealthy life script is an accident just waiting to happen. This same scernario can be applied to domestic violence siutations, juvenile gang situations, or even terroristic groups. TA training can be helpful in pinpointing the origin of personal biases, group prejudices, integrity issues, dark side leadership and organizational injustices.

As a personality theory, TA provides us with a means of understanding where toxic thoughts, attitudes, and behaviors were learned. As a training tool, TA, can help individuals, citizens, leaders, and police become more aware of themselves and the source or cause of their negative behavior.

Interaction Among Parent –Child- Adult Ego States

Below is an illustration of the three ego states. If A is conversing with B, and A speaks to B using communication characteristic of a parent and B replies using communication characteristic of the child ego state; then, a conflict may arise because the parent ego state represents rules learned without questions asked; and the child's ego state represents emotions aimed at having their way. In law enforcement, one can see how a citizen may interpret the directive of a police officer as disrespect or vice versa based on the police being an authoritarian figure using a parent ego state. The citizen may perceive that they are being spoken to not as an adult but as a child. The diagram below represents a parent – child transaction.

See Figure: **Transactional Analysis – Parent –Child- Adult Ego State(s)**

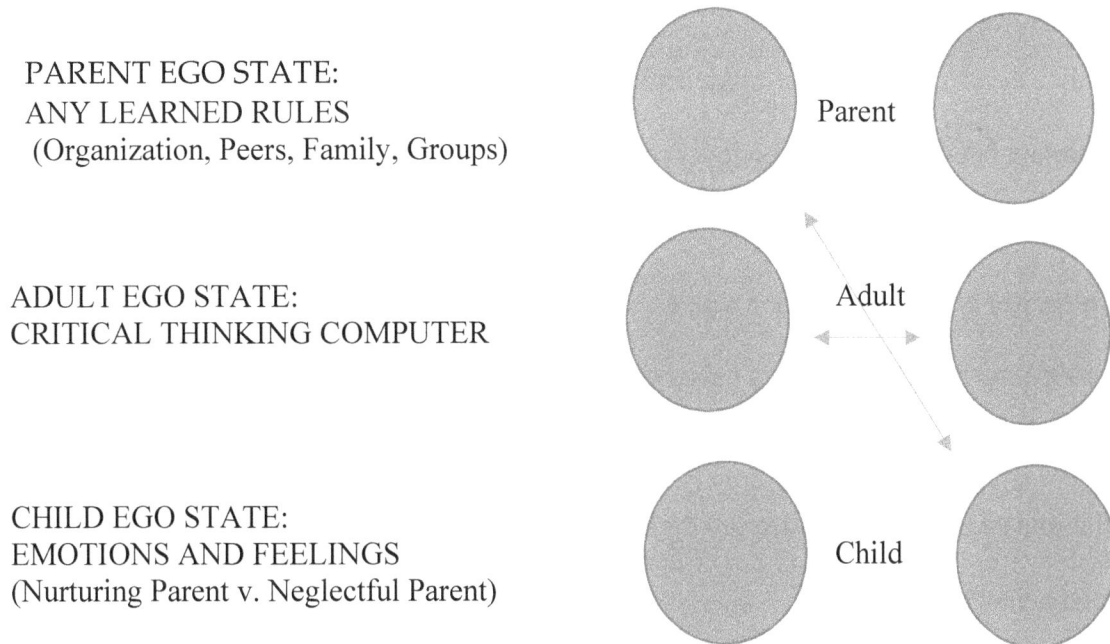

PARENT EGO STATE:
ANY LEARNED RULES
  (Organization, Peers, Family, Groups)

Parent

ADULT EGO STATE:
CRITICAL THINKING COMPUTER

Adult

CHILD EGO STATE:
EMOTIONS AND FEELINGS
(Nurturing Parent v. Neglectful Parent)

Child

Source: Harris (2004)

Another way of differentiating between the three ego states of one's personality is to

think of the parent ego state as information that has been taught to us. In the case of the child ego state,

it represents our experiences and the emotions associated with thoese experiences. As for the adult ego

state, it represents our update computer which allows us to delete obsolete information and add more

accurate information. Ideally, we should operate in the adult ego state because its' grounded in logic.

As a tool, TA empowers our self awareness. Another tool that helps us understand ourselves are our

mental models. Our mental models are closely related to our life scripts. In essence, our mental

models be can viewed as our own self-portrait and how we view the world.

XI. Mental Models

Mental models can be applied to organizations as well as individuals. Because trust is based on our interactins with others, it can represents a relationship that the community can have with the police as an institution. For organizational leaders, understanding the dimensions of trust is important because they are the focal point of their organizations (Weick, 1995). With respect to police community relations, citizens often pay a great deal of attention to what those in positions of power or authority do and say, as well as what they do not do and do not say (Kramer, 1996). As mentioned, police have been socialized to a certain world view based on their profession. While the "We" versus "Them" mentality raises serious concern with respect to its potential impact on how the police see their jobs and how the police do their jobs, it is part of their learned behavior.

Senge (1990) defined mental models as an individual's explanation or understanding of how something (culture) works. In today's society, race, gender, background, age, education, rural, urban, and income are all factors that may influence a person's view of the world. Because of cultural differences, each one of us can be inherently bias based on our experiences in contrast to someone else's cultural different. Without having the opportunities to examine these differences, we can act bias without thinking we are. When the issue is raised that we may be acting bias and we ignore it; then, we may use a defense mechanisms to cover up this information because we don't see ourselves that way.

Overcoming Defense Mechanisms

To overcome defense mechanisms, Senge(1990) recommended more openness. In order to narrow the gap between what we think the world should be like versus what the world actually is. Senge suggested the following tools can be used to better understand and challenge our view(s) of the world:

- o Leaps of Abstraction

- o Exposing the Left Hand Column

- o Balancing Inquiry with Advocacy

- o Espouse Theory v. Theories in Use

Briefly, Senge (1990) explained Leaps of Abstraction as the occurrence when an individual jumps from an observation to a generalization without verifying the data. For example, all police are corrupt or all black people want is welfare. These are sweeping generalizations void of any proof. The harm in these generalizations is that we decide to

treat all people in that category the same. Sense suggested another strategy for reducing our biases called exposing the left column. Senge understood that human beings store experiences in their memory and that 10 percent of what we know is conscious while the other 90 percent is unconsciously stored away. Exposing the left column is an exercise that forces us to think about what we didn't say and write it down.

Next, Senge uses the technique of balancing inquiry and advocacy. Balancing inquiry and advocacy means blending our ability to learn from others and our willingness to share our views and reasons with others. I remember having a conversation with a police captain regarding a policy issue. I instructed him to criticize my position which he did. However, when I responsed to his position with factual data, the dialogue stopped! Think about how many opportunities to solve problems are aborted because someone refuses to accept verified facts. Lastly, Senge uses two fancy terms called espouse theory and theories in use. In plain English, espouse theory is what we say out loud to others. Whereas, theories in use is what we actually do. For example, I tell my wife that I will be fateful to her but when I'm suppose to be working late – I'm out with my girlfriend. So much for the drama.

Senge used espouse theory and theories in use to show the contradiction between what we say and what we do. These contradictions and inconsistencies lead others to question whether or not we can be trusted. Senge suggested that the above skills will help us better understand our view of the world and the assumptions that go along with our views. These strategies will enable us to challenge how we look at the world and forces us to consider the world view of others.

Exercise

A possible mental model training exercise to illustrate our differences in world views could be demonstrated by using three groups: Group A consist of police officers, Group B consist of citizens, and Group C consist of both police and citizens. The groups will be asked to identify the traits of an "idea" police leader. The result of the exercise should confirm that no list of attributes are identical. While this past chapter dealt with how we view the world, the next chapter will focus on what happens to our body when our mental outlook is influenced by toxic thinking.

XII. Toxic Thoughts by Dr. Caroline Leaf

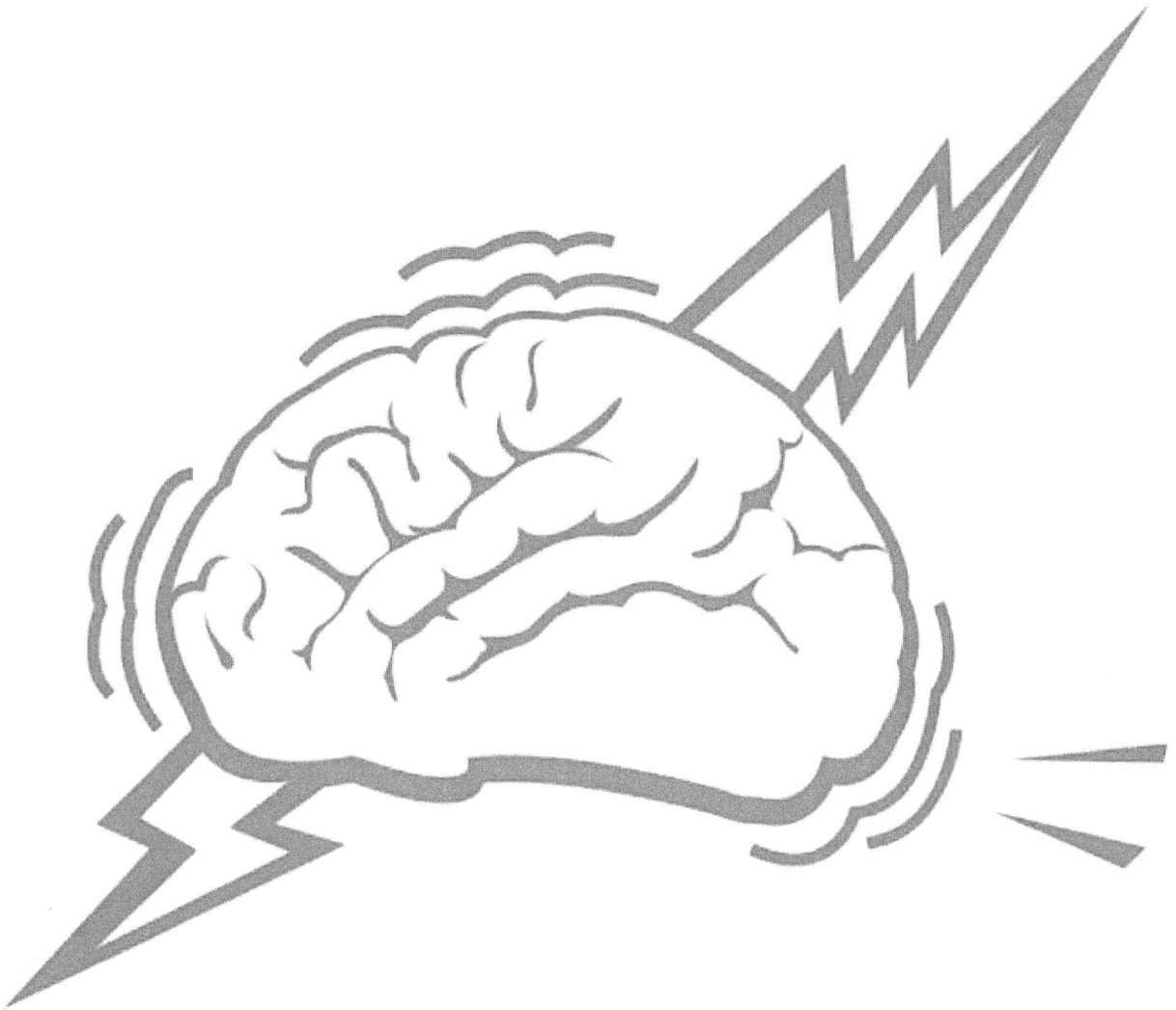

God's Word

According to the bible, God has not given us a spirit of fear, but of power and of love and of a sound mind. 2 Timothy 1:7. According to Dr. Caroline Leaf, your thought processes tell your mind what to do. Your thinking creates thoughts that are made out of proteins which constitute mental real estate. Our thinking instructs our brain to tell our body how to react. Therefore, if we control our reactions to external situations, we can influence our mind. Before moving forward, understanding and applying this point by Dr. Leaf can be a game changer. It can be the difference between winning and losing. In the foreward of this training manual, I referenced two great R&B song titles: Inner City Blues (Marvin Galye) and Living for the City (Stevie Wonder). While the songs pinpoint my history, we can go back to the song Strange Fruit (Nina Simone) or we can go contemporary with No Body's Smiling (Common) or Living Like Your Bullet Proof (Raheem DeVaugh). The point made in the lyrics of these songs is that the external conditions that minorities face has not changed much. In fact, Dr. Claud Anderson, in Powernomics, does a phenomenal job in detailing the historical conditions of black economic growth. So what's my point? If the external conditions have not changed; then, we must change our internal conditions or our thought processes to reach our true potential.

Toxic Thoughts

Research shows that 75 to 98 percent of mental, physical, and behavioral illness comes from one's thought processes. This staggering and eye-opening statistic means only 2 to 25 percent of mental and physical illnesses come from the environment and genes. Dr. Leaf stated that seventy five percent to ninety percent of the illness that affects us are a direct result of how we think. How we think affects us both physically and emotionally. Science shows that our thoughts and our feelings are a switch that turns certain genes on and off. Our experiences become the source of how we view the world and make sense of it. In general, negative experiences create negative feelings and a negative thought process. The same process holds true for positive experiences.

According to Dr. Leaf, we have a choice in terms of how we respond to negative events. Below is a decision chart illustrating how our choices can affect our health, disposition, and perspective. Figure _____.

Thought Process Decision Chart:

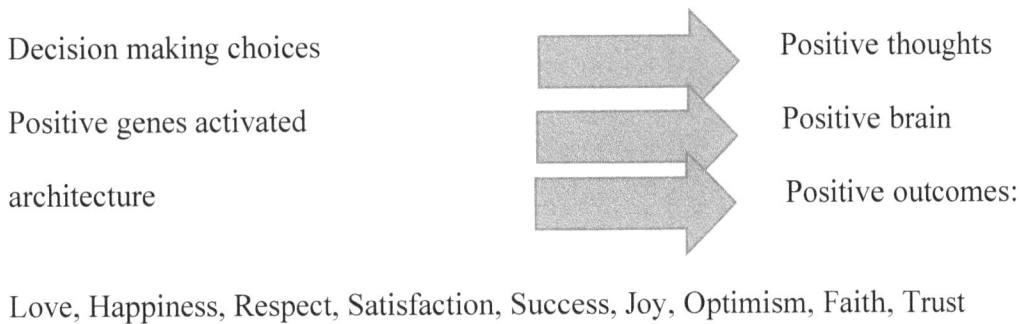

Decision making choices

Positive genes activated

architecture

Positive thoughts

Positive brain

Positive outcomes:

Love, Happiness, Respect, Satisfaction, Success, Joy, Optimism, Faith, Trust

_____   OR   _____

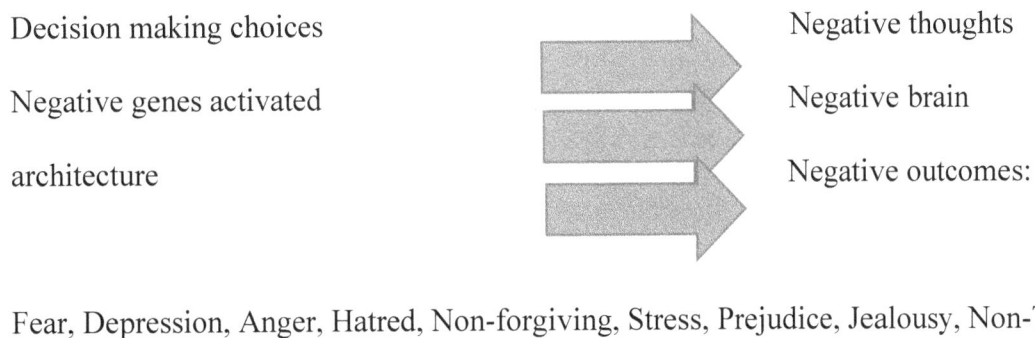

Decision making choices

Negative genes activated

architecture

Negative thoughts

Negative brain

Negative outcomes:

Fear, Depression, Anger, Hatred, Non-forgiving, Stress, Prejudice, Jealousy, Non-Trust

Dr. Jay 9-16-14

Summary of Dr. Leaf's research findings:

1. The debate in science is between the mind being what the brain does versus the brain doing the bidding of the mind.

2. The correct view is that the mind is designed to control the body, of which the brain is a part, not the other way around.

3. Our brain does not control us; we control our brain through our thinking and choosing.

4. We can control our reactions to anything.

5. Choices are real. You are free to make choices about how you focus your attention, and this affects how the chemicals, proteins, and wiring of your brain change and function.

6. Research shows that *DNA actually changes shape in response to our thoughts.*

7. Stress stage one is normal. Stress stage two and stage three, on the other hand, are our mind and body's response to toxic thinking—basically normal stress gone wrong.

8. *Reaction* is the key word here. You cannot control the events or circumstances of your life, but you can control your reactions.

In terms of the present training, police officers encounter accumulated amounts of stress over the course of their careers. As such, prolonged amounts of stress can influence the architecture of the brain and limit its nature capacity to process information in an optimal fashion. The good news is that positive thoughts can offset negative ones and restore the mind and body to a healthy state. The choice of taking control of our mind is up to each of us. It is the only thing that we truly control anyway; external conditions may influence us, but shouldn't control us. In terms of wellness, both citizens and police can benefits from this information. The next section continues this dialogue by describing how the brain works under extreme stess and fear.

XIII. How the Brain Works under Stress

Understanding the Brain Under Stress

As stated by Dr. Leaf, toxin thoughts are the main cause for physical illments to one's body. This section provides an explanation of how extreme stress and fear can trigger an emotional response that can lead to violence. For police and citizens, this information is very valuable in preventing and escalating conflicts. As an occupation which subjects police to unanticipated danger, police are concerned with their survival; the first step on Maslow's Hierarchy of Needs. Citizens, too, when faced with danger or the perception of danger, are concerned with their survival needs. A police officer or a citizen's perception of danger (mental view) translates into an interpretation of what is happening. When two individuals sense fear, the brain automatically signals a "fight-flight syndrome" response. If one party fails to remove themselves legally and/or judiciously from the confronation, the confrontation may escalate and turn violent.

Police officers have always been trained to control and defuse confrontations as part of their survival training. What is new in this equation is bringing forth the concern that the "We" versus "Them" mentality can influences an officer's perception and behavior during stressful encounters with a citizen or a suspect. This is a concern that needs further discussion if building trust is a priority. By addressing this concern, police administrators can demonstrate their recognition of the community's negative perception of "We" versus "Them" mentality and demonstrate their receptiveness to working with the community to overcome this negative perception that continues to undermine trust building. The remaining portion of this chaper will address how the brain works during a "fight-flight situation".

Studies have shown that what we know about the "fight –flight syndrome" is controlled by the amygdala. The amygdala is the size of a peanut but overrides the cortex, the largest portion of the brain, during stressful or fearful encounters. Because we each carry a unique mental model or view of the world based on our experiences, personality, culture, environment, and/or exposure, our view of the world is different from others and can influence how we perceive a situation. When we are confronted with stress or fear, the brain emits neuro-chemicals to prepare us for a fight or flight decision. This is normal. However, because we are each different, our bodies behave differently based on our experiences and how we process fear and stressful situations. Due to traumatic situations and acculmulated stress, the brain releases higher dosages of cortisones which can result in diminished cognitive abilities.

This information is significant for police officers because of the day to day stress that they experience. It is also significant to citizens who live under stressful conditions daily. Current incidents, as well as, past negative incidents stored in an individual's memory can trigger the amygdala. In similar scenarios, soldiers can experience post trauma stress reactions based on current triggers that activate past stressful encounter(s). The following charts depicts the process commonly known as the "Amygdala Hijack".

Charting the Amygdala Hijack

The brain response to an emotional arousal can take two paths (direct and indirect). As stated, individuals have differ experiences (mental models or images); therefore, our perception and interpretation of a what we see or think we see may be different for each individual. This includes both police and citizens.

58

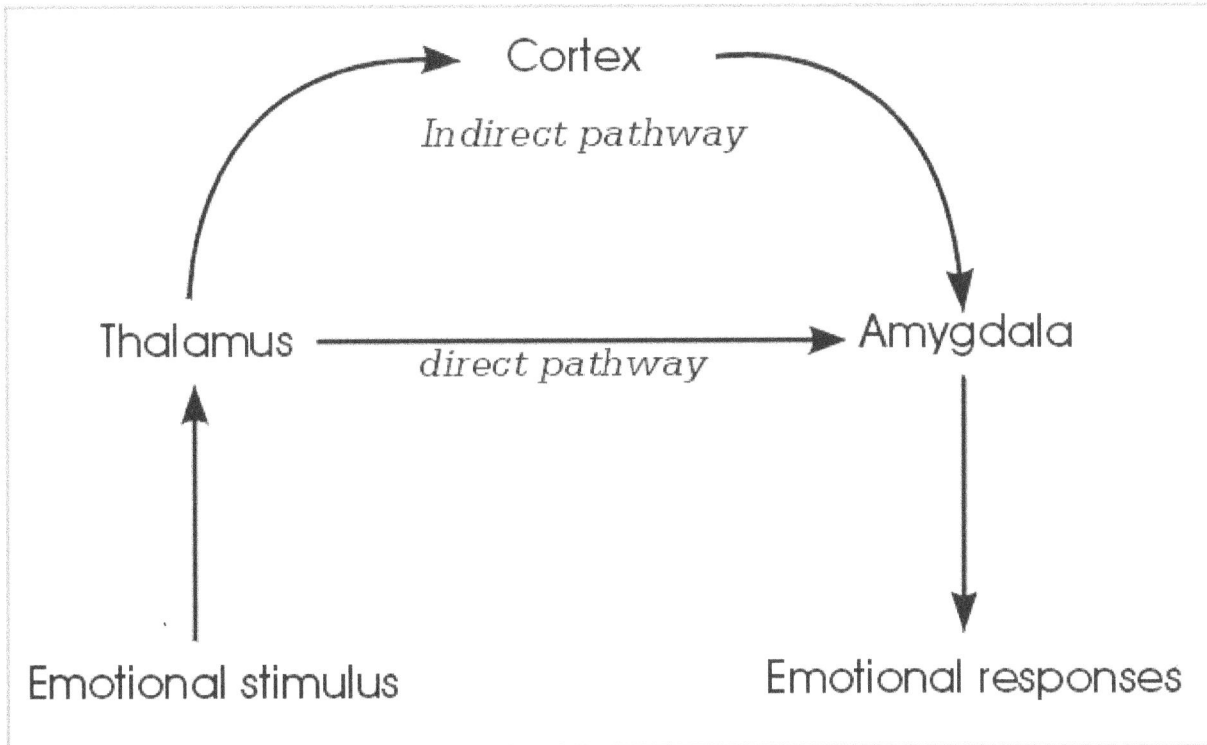

Fig 1: *Direct and indirect pathways to the amygdala.*

Source: J. LeDoux, *The Emotional Brain* (Phoenix (an Imprint of The Orion Publishing Group), London, 1999) as cited in Rimmele (2003).

The trade- off between the emotional stimulus taking the direct path over the indirect path is that the direct path provides a cruel incomplete representation of the stressful or fearful situation. Whereas, the indirect route takes longer but provides a more accurate assessment of the situation. From the perspective of the officer who is concerned with officer safety, time can be the different between life and death. However, from the perspective of a grieving loved one, a delay in the officer's actions to ascertain a better assessment of the situation is the preferred action to take. Life threatening events can occur within the blink of an eye; therefore, this type of training must be provided before events escalate. Integrating and balancing the concerns of the police for safety and those of a possible grieving mother is essential in building trust between the police and the community. These types of dialogue are long over due.

IVX. Emotional Intelligence

Based on our previous discussion, control over our emotions can be the different between living and dying. We all know individuals who: engaged in road rage, joke at an inappropriate times, continued to talk out loud during a movie, hate due to their racist views, exhibit jealousy and envy because of someone else's gift, or like to bully you. While these are all overt situations that we can all relate to, there are probably some underlying character flaws such as pride, selfishness, deceit, or feelings of inadequancy that possess individuals to behavior in these manners. Based on the confrontations and disputes that police are expected to resolve, emotional intelligence is essential. For the most part, the majority of officers do an outstanding job. However, there is always room for improvement with respect to the development of both police and citizens.

In working with emotional intelligence, Dr. Goleman (1998) coined the "amygdala hijack" term that was discussed in the previous section. A positive example of an "amygdala hijack" is when out of fear a 98 pound man can pick up a small car to free a trapped child. A negative example is when fear takes over and an expert police shooter freezes up and is unable to fire a shot at an armed bank robber. Fear triggers the "Fight – Flight" response and the emotional area of the brain turns off the analytical processing area of the brain. While there is a great deal of medical research on "amydala hijack", research linking it to police shooting or brutality cases is limited if any. The need for research in this area may be a project for an ambitious criminal justice major.

In terms of intelligent research, Dr. Howard Gardner (1983) introduced the theory that there are seven types of intelligence (language, math, kinesthelic, spatial, music, intra-personal, and interpersonal). Of these seven, Goleman (1998) focused on intra and interpersonal intelligence. Goleman defined interpersonal intelligence as the capacity to understand the intentions and behavior of others; while, he described intrapersonal intelligence as the capacity to better understand one self. To iterate, one premise of this training is that individuals need to know their own emotional strengths and weaknesses before they attempt to become an authority on someone else. EI attempts to provide such awareness.

Tools

According to Mayer and Salovey (1997), emotional intelligence can be used as a tool to help individuals to:

1. Perceive emotions – the ability to detect changes in emotions in faces, pictures, voices, and cultural artifacts—including the ability to identify one's own emotions.
2. Use emotions – the ability to use emotions in an appropriate manner to motivate learning and problem solving.
3. Understand emotions – the ability to comprehend emotion language of others and to use this understanding to improve relationships.
4. Manage emotions – the ability to regulate emotions in both ourselves and in others. More importantly, emotional intelligence teaches us how to take control over our own emotions (pp.3-31).

Competences

In addition, Goleman (1998) further identified the following emotional competencies that one should acquire from emotional intelligence training:

o Self-Awareness

o Self-Regulation

o Motivation

o Empathy

o Social Skills

For Police and Community members, the following sub-skills include: emotional awareness, accurate self-assessment, self-control, trustworthiness (standards of honesty and integrity), taking responsibility for one's own actions, understanding others, developing others, meeting customer needs, open to other cultures, understanding a communities political struggle, ability to listen, nurturing relationships, resolving conflicts, and formulating collective goals (Goleman, 1998). In addition, TalentSmart (2001-2014) further refines emotional intelligence training into the following four areas: self-awareness, self-management, social awareness, and relationship management. As a component of this training, participants can receive a confidential emotional intelligence appraisal to determine their baseline EI for a fee via www. TalentSmart.com. They also provide group discount rates.

Overcome Defensive Tactics

Goleman (1998) noted that training is needed because individuals sometimes engage in defensive tactics such as minimizing facts, filtering out crucial information, rationalizing, sense making, and making excuses as a means of covering up or denying an emotional truth. Denying an emotional truth is a normal routine that individual engage in when ever they are faced with a need to change their behavior. These are some of the same defense mechanisms addressed by Argris and Schon (1978) with respect to inhibiting our learning process. One of the benefits of emotional intelligence is that it enhances our self-awareness of our own biases. This self-awareness should make us less prone to continue negative thoughts and negative behavior.

Exercise

The following exercise could be used to demonstrate the importance of emotional intelligence training in law enforcement. Suppose we formulate three groups: Group A consist of all police officers, Group B consist of all citizens, and Group C consist of both police and citizens. In this particular exercise, the groups will discuss their emotions and how to handle a situation where an officer is dispatched to a suspicious person call at a convenience store and arrived to find a teenager sitting on the curb with a gun. The officer doesn't know if the gun

is real or a toy. The officer tells the teenager to get up and the teen points the gun at the officer.

Describe your emotions and develop procedures for what you and your group decided to do. By

understanding ourselves first, emotional intellignece gives us an opportunity to try to understand

others.   The next section proposes 12 principles to influence personal growth.

XV. 12 Principles of Transformation

In completing the section on emotional intelligence, I ran across the Twelve Laws of

Karma by Lily of O'Sullivan as seen on Utube and thought these laws would be an excellent way

of showing how real change comes from the inside. This section reinforces the importance of

being true to thyself before we can be true to others. It touches on who we are as individuals

and who we are striving to become. In my experiences as a probation officer, parole officer, and

police officer, I have learned that most people act bad because they feel bad.

Within the capacity of a probation officer, the parole officer, and the police officer, my

role was to provide a service to someone who was deficient in some way or another. The broken

home, the single parent household, the abused child, the drug or alcohol addicted parent, and the

juvenile delinquent child were common themes in each case. And despite, my commitment to

help each individual, the effort never achieved the desired or expected results. And when a child

failed, I, just like everyone else, blamed the child. For years, I never suspected that maybe the

system was broke.

Today, I can unequivocally say that the criminal justice system is broke

and the deterrent model does not work. Despite its woes, the deterrent model has not been

successfully challenged.for three primarily reasons: (1) it uses a deficient model which blames

the individual for his or her underachievement, (2) it supports the stereotype of underachievement by providing deficient resources within certain communities, and (3) it produces a revenue stream for someone based on the alleged plight of the underachiever. In essence, society labels certain people underachievers and supports those labels by failing to provide adequate resources that would change the conditions that the alleged underachiever must over come.

For example, children and parents are often blamed for an education system that lacks adequate financial resources, the best teachers, and a stimulating curriculum. While these are institutional problems that the child has no control over, it is often easier to blame the child and the parent rather than to address the issue of inadequate funding. System thinking forces us to look beyond the deficit model and focus on the whole system. System thinking also informs us that our mental model influences our perception of the problem and how we define it. System thinkings forces each of us to challenge our ways of thinking in an effort to find an optimum solution for everyone involved. The insertion of the 12 law of karma or twelve principles of transformation is to emphacize the important of changing our internal thought processes instead of waitng for external conditions to change. Listed below are the 12 law of karma or the (12 principles of transformation):

As you sow, so shall you reap. The law of cause and effect says whatever you put into the universe is what comes back. If what we want is happiness, peace, friendship, and love; then, we should be happy, peaceful, and a loving friend **(Law of Cause and Effect)**.

Life doesn't just happen, it requires your participation. We are one with the Universe both inside and out. Whatever surrounds us gives clues to our inner state. Be and do yourself. Do what you want to have in your life **(Law of Creation)**. Your inner state is what's in your heart. To this, I would add ask yourself what is your purpose and what Gift has God given you.

A lot of the time, we spend countless hours trying to emulate someone else's gift.

What you refuse to accept, will continue for you. If what we see is an enemy or someone with a character trait that we find to be negative; then, we ourselves are not focus on a higher level of existence (**Law of Humility**). Until we admit that we have personal flaws or that we need help with selfishness, pride, deception, etc,; then, these flaws will they continue to follow us.

Wherever you go, there you are for us to grow in Spirit. It is we who must change and not the people, places, or things around us. The only given we have in our lives is ourselves and that is the only factor we have control over. When we change who and what we are within our heart, our life changes too (**Law of Growth**). In discussing organizational change, Kotter and Cohen (2002) suggested that change with people is easier to achieve when people visualize the need and feel the urgency. Kotter and Cohen compared emotional oriented change to rational analytical change and stated that people are more susceptible to change when we appeal to their emotions rather than trying to persuade them solely by realms of data, logic, analysis, and report writing.

Whenever there is something wrong, there is something wrong with us. We mirror what surrounds us and what surrounds us mirrors us. We must take responsibility for what is in our life (**Law of Responsibility**). This law is similar to the law of attraction which states we attract negative people because we think negatively and vice versa. So if we see negative in others, its because we possess negative tendencies within our own character.

Even if something we do seems inconsequential, it is very important that it gets done as everything in the universe is connected. Each step leads to the next step and so forth and so on. Someone must do the initial work to get a job done. Neither the first step nor the last are of greater significance. They were both needed to accomplish the task, past, present, and future. They are all connected (**Law of Connection**). This law is very important because it suggest the idea of task continuity from one generation to the next. As such, humanity evolves based on our collective contributions. We must continue to teach a sense of purpose until the next generation learns their sense of purpose!

You can't think of two thnings at the same time. When our focus is on Spiritual Values, it is impossible for us to have lower thoughts such as greed or anger (**Law of Focus**). Oscillating between spiritual and devil oriented values reflects a gap in your integrity.

If you believe something to be true, then, sometime in your life. You will be called upon to demonstate that truth. Here is where we put what we say that we have learned into practice (**Law of Giving and Hospitality**). This law is about practicing with we preach or know. This law is about being consistent in applying what we know. It is another test of our integrity.

Looking back to examine what was, prevents us from being totally in the here and now. Olds thoughts, old patterns of behavior, old dreams… Prevent us from having new ones **(Law of Here and Now).** This law stresses the importance of learning forgiveness and moving forward.

History repeats itself until we learn the lessons that we need to change our path (**Law of Change**). One definition of learning is when our behavior changes for the better. We cannot grow until we change.

All rewards require initial toil. Rewards of lasting value require patient and persistent toil. True joy follows doing what we're suppose to be doing and waiting for the reward to come in its own time (**Law of Patience and Reward**).

You get back something whatever you've put into it. The value of something is a direct result of the energy and intent that you put into it. Every personal contribution is also a contribution to the Whole. Lack luster contributions have no impact on the Whole or work to diminish it. Loving contributions lift up and inspire the Whole (**Law of Significance and Inspiration).** This law reminds us that when we do our very best not only does it contribute to society and mankind, it also inspires others.

In a number of these laws, the concepts like the whole, of being all connected, of reaping what you sow, and of seeing the negative in others reflected a connection between the individual and his or her environment. These principles or laws were chosen because they relate to the concept of system thinking which emphacizes that our relationships are interdependent and part of a larger operating system. While most people see themselves as different, we really have more in common than what we think. The only thing that make people different are the different conditions that they live in or live through.

In law enforcement, the police have developed the "We" versus "Them" mindset that drives a wedge between them and some of the communities that they serve. This results in a lack of trust on both parts. The 12 laws of karma or 12 principles of transformation focus on developing your personal trust, integrity, and character. In addition, the 12 principles should challenge each individual not to wait for ideal conditions because those ideal conditions may never come. Use the 12 principles along with what your creator has already placed in you and move forward. The following section discusses procedural justice strategies as a means of building community trust between the police and the community.

XVI. Procedural Justice and Organizational Trust

Unlike the previous sections that focus on individual responsibilities, this chapter focuses on organizational responsibilities. Procedural justice is concern with fair procedures and fair treatment. In several police studies, Tyler and Folger (1980), found that reactions to encounters with police officers, teachers, and politicians were influenced by how authority figures followed procedures and how the individuals were treated. In a similar court and police study, Lind and Tyler (1988) found that parties to ligitation that received unfavorable outcomes reacted more favorable if the procedures were fair. For police, these findings are significant because fair procedures and fair treatment resonated well with citizens. In addition to fair procedures and fair treatement, procedural justice also advocates that employees and citizens should have input in the decision making process that pertains to their concerns. Kouzes and Posner (2002) added a procedural justice note that may make police administrators cringe when employees are allowed to challenge the status quo.

Despite this research, police still encounter trust issues with many of the communities that they serve. This author strongly believes that the "We" versus "Them" mentality contributes to this lack of trust. During my research on the code of silence, participants cited examples of mandatory reporting policy situations which were rendered ineffectiveness because of retaliation for violating the informal cultural practice (code of silence). This same scenario could be applied to the "We" versus "Them" mentality. The similarity between the code of silence and the "We" versus "Them" mentality is that they are both treated as "taboo" by police administrator. As mentioned earlier, ignoring these cultural taboos create an integrity issue for police administers.

The failure to address the "We" versus "Them" mentality with a policy initiative contradicts the procedural justice principles of due process and the fairness ensured to all participants. What assurance does the community have that the police will treat them fairly if no policies or procedures exist in these areas? How do they hold the police accountable? Below is a list of procedures that ensure fairness.

Fair Treatment and Procedures

As a guidepost, Leventhal (1980) and Tyler and Bies (1989) described fair treatment as (a) considering others' views, (b) suppressing personal bias,(c) consistency in decision application, (d) providing timely feedback, and (e) providing an adequate explanation. In addition, Leventhal (1980) suggested there are at least six procedural rules that individuals can use in judging fairness.

The six procedural rules are: (a) procedures that are consistent across individuals and are consistence over time, (b) decisions that are grounded on good information and informed opinion, (c) opportunities in place that can be used to modify or reverse decisions based on inaccurate information (correctability), (d) allocation processes that represent the concerns of all important subgroups and individuals (e) allocation processes that are compatible with prevailing moral and ethical standards, and (f) no personal self- interest and blind allegiance (politics). A department can apply these six rules to all its' procedures. In addition, the Department of Justice is a strong proponent of procedural justice strategies that promote fariness, citizen participation, and police neutrality (Tyler, 2004).

Conclusion-Training Exercise

Despite the information gleaned from procedural justice research, there exist far to many instances of discrepancies between what the written policies say and what the police culture allows. As a training exercise, develop three groups: Group A consist of all police officers, Group B consist of all citizens, and Group C consist of both police and citizens. The objective of this exercise is to develop a set of policies and procedures that address the "We" versus "Them" mentality in law enforcement. Compare the results of all three groups and discuss. The next section of the training will focus on dispute resolution and cooperative learning.

XVII. Dispute Resolution and Cooperative Learning

In conjunction with procedural justice principles, the fair handling of disputes between officers and citizens can greatly reduce some of the internal affairs complaints that the police departments currently receives. Several suggestions for conducting successful dispute resolutions included: a) active listening, b) avoidance of the "I" expression and more use of the "Our, Us, or We" expressions, c) showing empathy, d) managing your emotions, and e) reframing the issue (Frazer, 2010; Goleman, 1998; Covey, 2006; and Ryan & Oestreich, 1991).

With respect to reframing the issue, the solution posed should reflect a compromise or something that benefits both parties. In most disputes, we have been taught that someone has to win and someone has to lose. This is a carry over of our adversarial legal system. In this training, the author advocates a "win" "win" strategy for citizens and police. This approach is more in line with system thinking and cooperative learning.

As a tool, cooperative learning places an emphasis on: a) learning to work together b) personal responsibility for one's task, c) sharing the same goal(s), and d) measuring success by a win-win solution. Cooperative learning mirrors principles of system thinking which include: examining interdependent relationships, examining behavior within its context, finding complements, accepting responsibility for our faulty thinking, openness, and recognition of defensive mechanisms. Cooperative learning also mirrors procedural justice principles aimed at valuing employee and citizen input toward the goal of co-producing joint solutions.

In terms of building trust, cooperative learning can provide openness, collaboration, shared values, shared vision, and mutual benefits that forge strong relationships between the police and the communities they serve. The next section illustrates how this training can enhance an individual's personal, group, and societal development. Below is a development chart:

Diagram 1: Charting our Personal Development

System Thinking

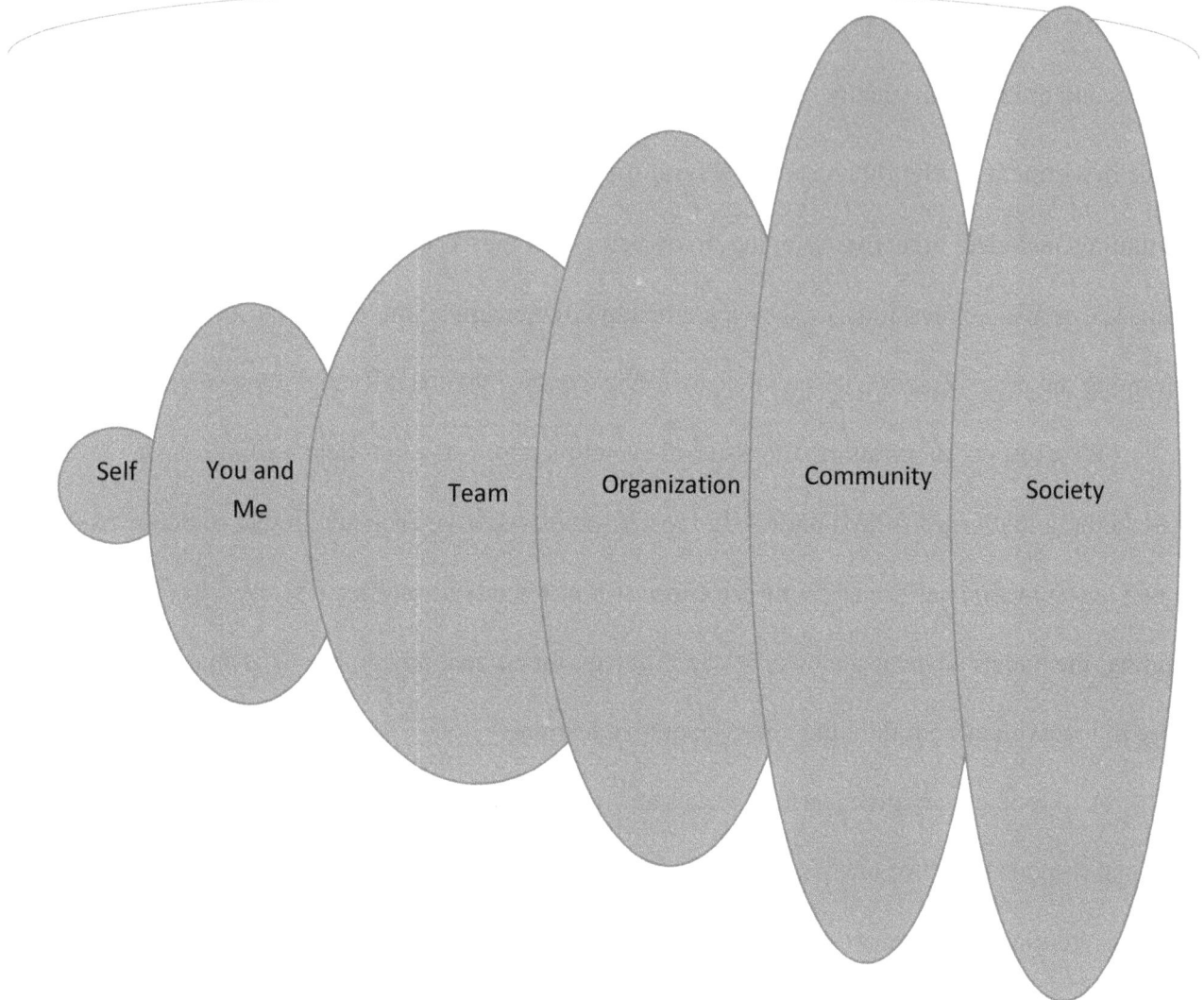

Self: (Negative Self-Esteem, Self-Portrait, Defense Mechanisms, Toxic Thoughts, Pride, Selfishness, Deception, Ulterior Motives, Jealousy, Personal Mastery, Mental Models, Personal Trust, Intrapersonal, 12 Keys of Karma)

You and Me: (Transactional Analysis, Emotional Intelligence, Conflict Resolution)

Team: (Shared Values, Shared Vision, Team Building, Conflict Resolution)

Organization: (Shared Values, Shared Vision, Procedural Justice, Cooperative Learning)

Community: (Shared Values, Shared Vision, Conflict Resolution, Cooperative Learning)

Society: (Shared Values, Shared Vision, Cooperative Learning)

Dr. Jay 9-16-14

XVIII. Post Training Exercise

Upon completion of the discussion on educational material on toxic thoughts, mental models, almygdala hijack, negative trust behaviors, fear preventative behaviors, transactional analysis, emotional intelligence, 12 principles of transformation, fair procedures, dispute resolution and cooperative learning, the three original teams will be evaluated by the group.

First, the instructor will call up the three teams that participated in the trust building role playing skits. The purpose of the post training exercise is to determine whether the educational information provided changed participants thinking and behavior. Participants will re-inact their role playing skits to reflect how the material helped them solve their problem. The duration of the second skit should be about 5-7 minutes; same as the first. While the teams are discussing their roles, the trainer will pass out the trust performance evaluation sheet to the group. The group will be asked to check-off items that they observed in the skit that are trust related and to write a one sentence explaination. Upon completion of the trust evaluation, the class will discuss what they observed. The instructor will allocate 15 minutes for the group discussion.

After group discussions, each group member will participate in a self evaluation. Group members will use the trust building questionnaire given to them at the start of the workshop and the trust performance evaluation sheet to compare their own responses to the trust performance checklist. After conducting this self-evaluation, a brief discussion will be held regarding the results. In concluding the training, the instructor will ask participants for suggestions to improve the training and also thank them for their participation.

IXX. Trust Performance/Evaluation Checklist

In this section, Covey (2006) identified thirteen strategies that build high-trust work environments. These strategies reflect both the interpersonal intelligence which deals with the capacity to understand the intentions and behavior of others and intrapersonal intelligence which deals with the capacity to understand one's self. As such, these strategies will also serve the performance/evaluation checklist. The performance/evaluation checklist is listed Below :

a) Straight talk: Yes _____ No _____
   Comments:_____

b) Demonstrate respect: Yes _____ No _____
   Comments: _____

c) Create transparency: Yes _____ No _____
   Comments: _____

d) Right wrongs: Yes _____ No _____
   Comments: _____

e) Show loyalty: Yes _____ No _____
   Comments: _____

f) Deliver results: Yes _____ No _____
   Comments: _____

g) Get better: Yes _____ No _____
   Comments: _____

h) Confront reality: Yes _____ No _____
   Comments: _____

i) Clarify expectations: Yes _____ No _____
   Comments:_____

j) Practice accountability: Yes _____ No _____
   Comments: _____

k) Listen first: Yes _____ No _____
   Comments: _____

l) Keep commitments: Yes _____ No _____
   Comments: _____

m) Extend trust: Yes _____ No _____
   Comments: _____

Source: Covey (2006) , Speed of Trust

Modified on 9-22-14 by Dr. Jay to include checklist and comment format.

XX. Leadership Development and System Thinking

According to Delattre (2011), public trust of the police was not based solely on what the police communicate to the public but how they performed their job(s). How police do their jobs has more to do with character than any other attribute. By character, I mean integrity. Covey (2006) listed the four personal trust components as: a) integrity, b) real motives, c) capacities, and d) results. Covey defined integrity as the congruence between what a leader says and what a leader does. Among the four trust attributes, integrity is the most important for a leader. As with police community relations, leaders must demonstate trust and integrity in order to be effective. Organizational integrity refers to what the organization does and what it says.

In describing leadership behavior associated with the code of silence, Trautman (2007), stated that 73% of officers admitted they were pressured by their boss to remain silent. This kind of pressure reflected an incongruence or a contradiction between department policies and the leader's actions. In terms of addressing the "We" versus "Them" mentality, the traditional police response has been to ignore it. Both the code of silence and the "We" versus "Them" mentality are artifacts of police cultural DNA; yet, police administrators fail to acknowledge these problematic issues throught policy initiatives. Using Trautman's research as an example, the failure to acknowledge the "We" versus "Them" mentality not only contradicts a number of best practices such as community trust building, effective leadership, procedural justice, and creating a healthy organization. The lack of effective leadership is a problem that cascades down the ranks and rendering the organization ineffective.

In layman's terms, let's say that I am a car sales man and I know that I am selling you a car with a defective engine, and I tell you how every thing else is beautiful about the car but conceal the fact that the engine is defective due to water damage.

What have I just done? At the very least, I have misrepresented and failed to disclose a problematic issue that I was privy to but failed to share with you (the customer). This situation parallels situations when police administrators fail to acknowledge and address problemation cultural norms such as the code of silence or the "we" versus "them" mentality. By engaging in deferred maintainence, covering up on going problems, and/or engaging in impression management strategies; sooner or later, the public will find out and come to the conclusion that the police lack integrity and cannot be trusted. Unfortunately, by the time that the public finds out, the problem has become more difficult to management and more costly. In previous sections, examples of negative trust behaviors were illustrated. Next, Covey described some attributes of a healthy trust oriented organization. Using this list, how well does your organization measure up?

Characteristics of a Healthy Trust Organization

With respect to organizations, Covey (2006) defined a healthy organization as one with the following trust characteristics: 1) sharing information openly, 2) promoting an innovative culture, 3) respecting those not present, 4) meaningful communication and collaboration, 5) people are praised and given credit for their contributions, 6) there is little or no backstabbing 7) transparency is the norm, 8) people value honesty, 9) there is a high degree of accountability, and 10) people are motivated about the mission. Overall, companies that engage in the above practices are more productive and innovative than their counterpart. The next section matches the characteristics of a healthy organization to idea leadership characteristics. Again, the gap between saying and doing remains the litmus test for any administrator. As previously stated, the Police Chief is the responsible for shaping the police culture. The following characteristics are some attributes of effective police leaders.

Characteristics of Effective Police Leaders

In conjunction with developing strong leaders, Schafer (2008) described an effective police leaders as possessing the following traits (a) demonstrating trustworthiness, (b) decision-making input, (c) admitting mistakes, (d) making informed decisions based on research, (e) fair treatment of all employees, and (f) allowing employees discretion to manage responsibilities within their skill set. With respect to building trust, these leadership characteristics apply to officers as well as police administrators. The next section considers the need for a possible leadership role change to better facilitate a trust building environment.

Role of a System Thinking and Learning Organizational Leader

Historically, policing was influenced by the bureaucratic thinking associated with Max Weber, who characterized bureaucracies as being hierarchical, specialized, impersonal, and rule oriented. While this section will not attempt to list the pitfalls associated with this form of organizing, one of the most obvious barriers to organizational learning in police organizations is the lack of market competition. As a business model, police organizations are like monopolies. Police have found a degree of success in using the deterrent model and have ignored other alternatives. Because alternatives have not been introduced, the police culture repeats itself as a matter of default.

In terms of leadership succession, this point is significant because irregardless of who the police chief is, unless he or she is up to the task of changing the values of the police culture; then, police behavior based this mindset will revert back to the norm. While a number of leadership practitioners have advocated a change in leadership style from autocratic to participatory management, others have suggested more in line with a learning oganization.

In a learning organization, Senge (1990) described the role of the leader as different from the traditional authoritarian role identified with most police departments. Senge described the traditional role to include managing, organizating, and controlling. In contrast, the role of a learning organization leader is that of a designer, teacher, and steward. The designer is responsible for creating the organization's vision, mission, policies, strategies, structures and monitoring the organization's learning process. The teacher's role is to monitor the employee's perspective regarding how things work and to examine the assumptions that influence their decisions. And last, the steward was defined as a leader who is committed to a higher set of values, empowering others and committed to building a better organization irregardless who gets the credit. Among these roles, the designer is charged with the responsibility of changing the existing model when it becomes ineffective and dysfunctional.

The Leadership Challenge

The role of the leader is always to model the way (Kouzes & Posner, 2002) rather than allow the culture to dictate the norms of the organization (Schein, 2004). How will police leaders address the "We" versus "Them" mentality? While recruitment, cultural diversity, and police community dialogue are important strategies; unless, police change or complement the existing deterrent model with a systems approach and systemic thinking, no real change will ever occur. Because the "We" versus "Them" mentality is part of the culture, police leaders must "unlearn" police officers before they can "relearn" them to a new theoretical framework (system approach). The section below explains why a systems approach and system thinking are the necessary tools for police reform and trust building.

System thinking is a suitable approach to addressing the "We" versus "Them" mentality because it seeks to understand and to balance the dual roles of protecting the rights of victims and protecting the rights of the accused (Gharajedaghi, 2006). While system thinking seeks to find complements among opposites, its' purpose is to understand why certain patterns of behavior are systemic. In order to accomplish this, it focuses on the interdependent relationships and the needs of both parties. For leaders, the most challenging aspect of system thinking is accepting responsibility for the internal policies and procedures that contribute to the problem as opposed to blaming the operational ineffectiveness on external factors (Richmond, 2001). At present, the "We' versus "Them" mentality prohibits a shared image of the police and community working together because it conflicts with many of the originate values of policing conceived by Sir William Peel. As a complement to the existing deterrent model, system thinking offers a fresh perspective on addressing police community trust building. The next section proposes a blue print for institutionalizing police community relations

XXI. Blue Print for Institutionalizing Police Community Relations

As indicated, the need for police reform can be due to personnel issues, policy issues, compliance issues, or implementation issues. However, at the center of police reform, leadership is the common denominator. What differentiates this training from other training is that its' aimed is to assist individuals, police, management, leaders, suspect (s) or citizens, to enhance their awareness of themselves prior to interacting with others. By enhancing their intrapersonal skills, the assumption is that one's interpersonal skills will also improve. In this sense, the training is integrated and holistic. This training does not only help individuals make better decisions but it should help them assess situations before decisions are made. The training is part of a system's approach to creating an organization or social structure design that meets the needs of police and community members.

Designing a Systems Model for Instituting Effective Community Policing

The following conceptual framework proposes a self –regulating model to reform police culture and institutionalize community policing. In order to do this, the following components are incorporated in this blue print: Organizational Philosophy, Organizational Values, Organizational Goals/Objectives, Performance Process Design, Performance Indicators, Performance Evaluation Tools (Qualitative, Quantitative, Audits), Commander Balance Scorecard, Best Practice Perspective, Learning Perspective, Internal Process Perspective, Customer Perspective, and Financial Perspective.

Changing Police Culture

Organizational Core Values	Organizational Philosophy	Organizational Goals/Objectives
Protect and Perserve Life	Community Policing	Decease Crime
Transparency Builds Trust	Note: Current "We" vs.	Arrest Rates, Clearance, COMPS
Constant Improvement	"Them" mentality	Increase Customer Satisfaction
	Implies Police are	Citizens Complaints, Procedural
	Inherently Bias	Justice, Building Comm. Trust

Performance Process Design	Key Performance Indexs	Evaluation Services

---

Define Organizational Outputs:	Functions:	Audit Behavior:
Units, Cost, Time Period,	Integrate Patrol/Investigation	Desired Behavior/Real Behavior
Quality, Feedback Survey	Services	Early Warning Signs
Define Success Behavior	Support Services	Determine Cause and Effect
Define Critical Success Steps	Dispatch, Forensics,	Correct via Recommendations
Evaluate Process Results	Property, Fleets, Tech.	Auditing Policy and Procedure
Determine Why Discrepancy	Organizational Learning	Alignment linked to Org. Goal
Exist	Services	Auditing Efficiency Ratio
Make Process Improvements	Planning and Research	Cost Same/Improve Service
	Best Practices	Cost Decrease/Service Same
	Training Police Academy	

Organizational Productivity

Commander's Balance Scorecard

Best Practices Perspective	Learning Perspective	Internal Process Perspective
Key Performance Indexes	Innovative Strategies	Assess the Cause and Effect
Each Functional Area	Improve Performance Process	Process of Performance
(Bench Marks)	Best Practices Training	Discrepancies With
	Police Academy	Emphasis on Why of The
		Cause

Customer Perspective	Financial Perspective
Focus on Customer	Bench Mark Cost Factors
Satisfaction	Focus on Efficiency Ratio
Feedback With Emphasis on	Reducing Crime
Building Trust	Increaseing Citizen Satisfaction
	Reducing Cost
	Increasing Citizen Trust

Evidence: Research, Quantitative, Qualitative, Narratives, Flow-Charts, etc.

Dr. Jay 8-17-14

REFERENCES:

Argyris, C. & Schon, D. (1978). *Organizational learning: A Theory of Action Perspective*, Ready, Mass. Addison Wesley.

Burton, L. (2014). *Get on the train or leave. lynsiburton@seattlepi.com*

Covey, S. M.R. and Merrill, R.R. (2006). *The Speed of Trust*. Free Press. New York.

Crank, J. P. (2004). *Understanding police culture* (2nd ed.). Cincinnati, OH: Anderson Publishing.

Delattre, E. J. (2011). *Character and cops: Ethics in policing*. Washington, DC: American Enterprise Institute for Public Policy Research.

Fraser, W. (2010). *Trust and repair: An exploration of how work groups repair a violation of trust.* Unpublished doctoral dissertation, Fielding Graduate University, Santa Barbara, CA.

Gardner, Howard (1983), *Frames of Mind: The Theory of Multiple Intelligences*, Basic Books.

Gharajedaghi, J. (2006). Systems Thinking. Boston, MA: Elsevier Publishing.

Goleman, D. (1998). *Working with Emotional Intelligence*. Bantam Books. New York

Harris, T. A. (2004). *I'm OK, You're OK*. Harper

Human Rights Watch (2012)

Ikerd and Walker (2010) Making Police Reform Endure: Institutionalizing Problem-Oriented Policing

International Association of Chiefs of Police. (1999). *Police leadership in the 21st century*. Retrieved on 10-2-2013 from http://www.iacp.org/Police-Leadership-in-the-21st-Century

Jensen, K. T., (2012). Ten Police Scandals.Source: http://www.mandatory.com/2012/06/19/the-10-biggest-police-scandals/

Kouzes, J. & Posner, B. (2002). *The Leadership Challenge*. San Francisco, CA. John Wiley & Sons

Kramer, R. M., & Lewicki, R. J. (2010). Repairing and enhancing trust: Approaches to reducing organizational trust deficits. *The Academy of Management Annals, 4*(1), 245–277.

Leaf, C. (2013). *Switch on Your Brain*. Grand Rapids, MI, Baker Books Publishing

LeDoux,J. (1999). *The Emotional Brain* (Phoenix (an Imprint of The Orion Publishing Group), London, 1999) as cited in Rimmele (2003).

Leventhal, G. S. (1980). What should be done with equity theory? In K. J. Gergen, M. S. Greenberg, & R. H. Willis (Eds.), *Social exchange* (pp. 27-55). New York, NY: Plenum.

Lind, E. A., & Tyler, T. R. (1988). *The social psychology of procedural justice*. New York, NY: Plenum.

Mayer, J.D., & Salovey, P. (1997). What is emotional intelligence? In P. Salovey & D. Sluyter (Eds.), *Emotional development and emotional intelligence: Implications for educators* (pp. 3-31). New York: Basic Books.

McIntosh, G. & Rima, S. (2005). *Overcoming the Dark Side of Leadership*. MI. Baker Books

New York Times (2012). EDITORIAL, August 8, 2012 Stop and Frisk in New York City

Richmond, B. (2001). An Introduction to Systems Thinking. High Performance Systems, Inc.

Rimmele, U. (2003). A Primer on Emotions and Learning

Ryan, K. D. and Oestreich, D.K. (1991). *Driving Fear Out of The Workplace*. San Francisco: Jossey-Bass Publishers.

Schafer, J. (2008). Effective police leadership: Experiences and perspectives of law enforcement leaders. *FBI Law Enforcement Bulletin, 77*(7), 13-19.

Trautman, N. E. (2007). *Integrity leadership*. (5th ed.). Springfield, IL: Charles C. Thomas Publisher, LTD.

Tyler, T.R. & Wakslak, C. J. (2004), Profiling and Police Legitimacy: Procedural Justice, Attributions of Motive, and Acceptance of Police Authority, *Criminology*, Vol. 42, Iss. 2,pages 253-282, May 2004.

Webster's Fourth Edition (2005). *Dictionary*.Wiley Publishing Inc. Cleveland, Ohio

APPENDIX: TRAINING MODULES

FEAR OF MAKING A MISTAKE CASE SCENARIO:

Themes:

Manipulating facts

Creating climate of fear

Practicing denial

Disrespectful behavior

Script:

Two officers respond to a suspicion person complaint. The dispatcher describe the allege suspect as having a green shirt and blue jeans, black male, earlier twenties, and running away from complainant's red brick home. Officers arrive eight minutes later and canvas neighborhood before going to speak with complainant. Officers observe a black male about age 50 on the same street with a blue shirt and blue jeans. Officers stop this individual and question him about what's he doing in the area. This individual told Officers that they were harassing him and he hadn't broken any laws. Officers detained this individual so that the complaint could identify him as the peeping tom. Complainant stated that the citizen was not the peeping tom. Officers released him. Citizen make an IAD complainant on officers for harassment. Officers responded by stating in their letters that suspect used vulgar language at them and that's why he was detained.

FEAR OF WITHDRAWAL OF FIELD SUPPORT CASE SCENARIO:

Themes:

Creating climate of fear

Not listening to others

Disrespectful behavior

"We" versus "Them" mentality

Script:

Two Officers are dispatched to a burglary in progress. Officers arrived but suspect is GOA. Officers located point of entry and canvas house for safety precautions. Upon canvassing house, officers notices a rolex watch on the bedroom room floor. Officer A decides to confiscate the watch as a personal memento. Officer B tells his partner to leave it and Officer A refuses. Later, in the car, Officer A tells Officer B that you don't want to be known as a "snitch".

FEAR OF MANAGEMENT, INCONSISTENCIES, UNFAIR TREATMENT, AND DISCIPLINARY CONSEQUENCES:

Themes:

Avoiding undiscussables

Creating climate of fear

Leader punishing critic

"We" versus "Them" mentality

Misalignment of intent and actions

Script:

While Officer Penrose checking by with the primary unit, Officer Johnson was apprehending a suspect for possession of marijuana. After the suspect was handcuffed, Officer Johnson struck suspect in the mouth for talking back. Suspect complained to IAD. Officer Penrose was contacted by IAD as a witness. Before he wrote his letter, Officer Penrose's supervisor told him that we all stick together. Officer Penrose perceived the sergeant's comments as a veiled threat to retaliation since he was on the sergeant's list for promotion.

FEAR OF BEING LABELLED A SNITCH

Themes:

Leader punishing critic

"We" versus "Them" mentality

Engaging in the blame game

Creating a climate of fear

Script:

Citizen Q observed the shooting in front of the deceased residence. The police arrived after suspect had fled. Police asked Citizen Q what she had seen. Citizen Q was assured that the police would protect her if she told them what she saw. Citizen Q stated that she remembered when another citizen eye witnessed a drug related shooting and that witnesses home was shot up. Citizen Q is unsure what to do.

FEAR OF NO DEPARTMENT PROTECTION

Themes:

"We" versus "Them" mentality

Creating a climate of fear

Leader punishing critic

Manipulating facts

Practicing denial

Misalignment of intent and actions

Script:

Sergeant T was informed of a complaint of sexual harassment that a subordinate made to him about his Captain. Sergeant T knew this was a sensitive situation so he asked the female subordinate to rescind her complaint against the Captain. The female subordinate told Sergeant T if he didn't make the complaint she would go directly to IAD. Sergeant T felt he would be retaliated against in the future by other Captains.

FEAR OF LAWSUITS

Themes:

Manipulating facts

Practicing denial

Misalignment of intent and actions

"We" versus "Them" mentality

Creating a climate of fear

Admitting a mistake

Script:

Chief Jones received an IAD investigation indicating that officers had poor intel and served the warrant on the wrong residence, and the injury sustained by the innocent complainant was a direct result of poor intelligence gathering from police informant. Chief Jones decides to cover up the mistake and tell the media that a high volume of drug trafficking occurs in the neighborhood in order to maintain loyalty to his officers.

FEAR OF DAMAGING LEADER'S REPUTATION

Themes:

 Manipulating facts

Practicing denial

Misalignment of intent and actions

"We" versus "Them" mentality

Creating a climate of fear

Admitting a mistake

Script:

Chief Robrowski was up for promotion to Assistant Chief when he found out that his vice squad was receiving kickbacks to allow prostitution to flourish without enforcement. The IAD captain wanted to take the matter over to the district attorney's office and schedule a grand jury. The chief said that the investigation needs to be minimized, delayed or go away.

FEAR OF TRANSPARENCY

Themes:

Manipulating facts

"We" versus "Them" mentality

False reporting

Script:

Citizen viewed an altercation where suspect who was hand cupped was kicked several times in the groin area after subdued. The suspect made an IAD complaint against officer and stated that you were the witness. The investigator contacted you as to what you observed. You are hesitate to offer your view of what happen because you believe that all police stick together and will cover up this matter. How would you persuade this reluctant citizen to participate in the IAD complaint process.

DEFINITIONS

Mental Models:

Mental models are the underlying assumptions or reasoning that motivates us to behavior a certain way. Mental models are how we look at the world.

Mental Maps:

Mental maps are similar to mental models in that they too are mental pictures of how we should act in certain situations.

Self-Portrait:

Self-portraits are how we look at ourselves based on our interaction with the world.

Learning organization:

A learning organization is part of a system which is designed to create its own future by learning to meet the needs of all interdependent components.

Single Loop Learning:

Single loop learning is when errors are detected in policies, rules, norms, and values and corrections are made in order to do a more efficient job. This is a form of adaptive learning which is reactionary. Knowledge is used to make the existing policies, rules, norms, or values more efficiency or effective. There is no change.

Double Loop Learning:

Double loop learning is when errors are detected in policies, rules, norms, and values; then, these governing variables are questioned. By questioning the policies, rules, norms, and values, a new set of values and norms are created to address problems in the organization. Generative learning utilizes what is already know with what is learned thought reflecting on the problem. As such, new knowledge is created. Change occurs.

Code of Silence:

The unwritten police practice of not reporting on the misconduct of a fellow officer.

"We" versus "Them" Mentality:

The police cultural view of the world is based on their socialization and their concern for safety.

System Thinking:

Viewing the components of a social system as a whole whose parts are interdependent.

Emotional History:

Our personal experiences both good or bad that can trigger (or be triggered) an emotional respond within a current or future relationship.

Integrity:

The absence of a gap between what you say that you're doing to do and what you actually do.

POST SCRIPT

All human beings have weaknesses. While we may not know all of them, it is our responsibility to learn them so we can be what God expects us to be. Whether our role in life be that of a police man or citizen, we all struggle will pride, selfishness, deception, and ulterior motives. These character traits are all a part of our dark side. McIntosh and Rima (2005) stated when we get offended because our ideas are rejected, or because we didn't receive the attention we felt that we deserve, or because a colleague out performed us, or because we felt someone didn't respect our title or authority; then, our anger, frustration, and jealousy is a reflection of our dark side. These negative feelings, whether known or unknown, to us (police or citizen) can be a manifestation of some unmet need (Maslow's Hierarch of Needs) in our past or in our present (McIntosh & Rima, 2005). Until we are willing to put in the work to offset our character flaws, we will never reach our full potential and achieve what God has already put in us. While the material set forth in this training manual is valuable to all individuals, it is extremely valuable to leaders. Today, there is a shortage of leaders who want to mentor their subordinates(s) into leadership positons. This manual may renew that commitment for some leaders.

BIBLIOGRAPHY

Dr. John "Jay" Hall is one of nine children. The only child who attended college. He grew up in Gary, Ind. - Chicago, Ill. and developed his grit from being one of the "corner boys". With some help from some decent cops, who saw his potential, he was encouraged to go to college. His academic achievements: B.A. Sociology and Criminology from Calumet College, M.A Public Administration from Indiana University, M.S.M. Management from Houston Baptist University, and Phd. Organizational Behavior, Management, and Leadership from Capella University, are accomplishments for his father, who served in the Navy, but still fled from Mississippi in order to give his family a better life, which I am immensely grateful for. As a baby bloomer, my mental model is still influenced by the civic rights struggle. To that extent, I am a strong proponent of social justice. However, I believe in teaching individuals how to fish rather than just giving them a fish. Its' part of the "tough love" campaign. Again, many thanks to Minister Kisha Jones for bringing this project to fruition.   Praise the Lord!

BACK BOOK COVER

Dr. John "Jay" Hall is a social engineer who seeks understanding of human behavior by studying across disciplines. His interest in system theory, organizational learning, and system thinking was piqued as a police practioner who saw reoccurring patterns of behavior without any changes in the criminal justice system. The absence of change in the criminal justice system has resulted in high recitivist rates with little or no prospect of social, economic, or political rehabilitation for offenders. The failure to rehabilitate offenders contributes to communities that, in turn, bred more social decay. Unless the law enforcement community is willing to change this current destructive trajectory, many law abiding citizens are subject to "collateral damage". System thinking advocates that linear thinking and how we define problems contributes to the very problems that we complaint about. System thinking embraces constructive voice in order to collectively design a system to produce constant operational harmony that works for all stakeholders.

Dr. John "Jay" Hall is the lead consultant at Leading with Integrity which focuses on system thinking training for police leaders.

www.ingramcontent.com/pod-product-compliance
Lightning Source LLC
Chambersburg PA
CBHW081420270326
41931CB00015B/3348